MANGER

to

MERCY

ALSO BY STEPHANIE RIPPLE

Off with the Old, On with the New:
A Biblical Guide to Cultivating Character in Your Children

A portion of all proceeds from the sales of
Off with the Old, On with the New and *Manger to Mercy*
will benefit Jennifer's Harbor.
www.jennifersharbor.org

MANGER

to

MERCY

Portraits of Grace
An Advent Devotional

STEPHANIE RIPPLE

ISBN: 979-8-9930051-0-2 (Paperback)
ISBN: 979-8-9930051-1-9 (Hardcover)
ISBN: 979-8-9930051-2-6 (eBook)

To Connie—
Neither this book nor my first would exist without your encouragement.
Whether you remember it or not, when I first shared this vision in its
rough, unformed, simple format, you spoke life into it. You made me
believe that, with God, I could actually bring it to fruition. You spoke with
gentle certainty, telling me I would be an author one day.

And I (eventually) believed you.

Oil and perfume make the heart glad,
so a man's counsel is sweet to his friend.
—Proverbs 27:9

Contents

Foreword

It is an honor to write these words for my dear friend, Stephanie Ripple. I have known Stephanie for many years, and over that time I have been blessed to walk alongside her in both the beautiful and the broken places of life. Through it all, one thing has remained constant: she is a true lover of Jesus Christ.

Stephanie abides in Him in a way that is both steady and beautiful. She places the Word of God at the highest standard, allowing Scripture to be the measure of truth and the anchor of her life. She pursues the will of God with wholehearted devotion, and she does so with integrity, humility, and a life marked by prayer. To know Stephanie is to know a woman of truth, grace, and unshakable faith.

Within these pages, you'll journey alongside men and women of Scripture who met Jesus face-to-face—Mary, Peter, the Samaritan woman, the Magi, and many others. Each devotion is a window into grace, pairing biblical truth with reflection and prayer that speaks into the everyday struggles of our own lives. Whether you come with joy or weariness, with questions or faith, these readings will gently draw your heart nearer to the Savior.

When I read this devotional, I was deeply moved. *Manger to Mercy: Portraits of Grace* is not just another book to add to your shelf—it is a guide that leads you closer to the heart of Christ. With each page, Stephanie invites you to pause, reflect, and encounter Jesus in a more intimate way. She writes not from theory but from a place of deep relationship with Him, and the result is a powerful devotional filled with timeless truths and tender reminders of God's mercy.

I believe this book will lead readers into a more personal and transformative walk with the Lord. It will help you quiet the noise, fix your eyes on Jesus, and see His grace more clearly in both the cradle and the cross.

It is with great joy that I commend this work to you. My prayer is that as you read these pages, you will experience what I have experienced not only through Stephanie's writing but through her life: the beauty of a soul fully surrendered to Christ and the power of His Word to change us from the inside out.

Deb King
Founder & Executive Director
Jennifer's Harbor

Preface

October 2022

A season of travel loomed ahead. A nine-hour drive to North Carolina to celebrate Thanksgiving with family. Nearly every weekend booked in a different city for my daughter's basketball games. Christmas planned in Cincinnati. All joyful, but the stress of the logistics weighed on my heart.

One morning, during a walk, I prayed.

"Lord, how in the world am I supposed to find time to put up a tree and all the decorations? Does it even make sense? All of our celebrations this year are away from home. I don't want to put up a tree!"

"*Don't.*"

"What?"

"*Don't put up a tree.*"

"But everyone always puts up a tree."

"*Simplify.*"

That quiet exchange got my wheels turning. When my kids woke up, I asked them, "On a scale of one to ten, how important is it to you that we put up a Christmas tree?"

To my surprise, they answered: one and zero. (I didn't even bother asking my husband—I already knew he'd register a negative on that scale.)

That settled it. I wasn't going to stress myself out over a tree. I was going to find contentment in doing things differently. But I wondered, *What about future Christmases?*

That year turned out to be glorious. The artificial tree we owned was enormous, too big for our house, really. We bought it as newlyweds, having no idea what we were doing. Every year, we would have to drag it down from the attic, piece by oversized piece, rearrange the entire living room, hauling furniture to the basement just to make space.

After that Christmas I no longer desired to make room for a tree; I desired to make more room for the Savior. And yet . . . I did love placing the ornaments. Each one held a memory—people, moments, stories. That part brought me joy. But one thing became clear: I never wanted to put up *that* tree again.

So, what would I do moving forward?

Shortly after that exchange with the Lord, He planted an idea in my heart—a new kind of Christmas display. One that wouldn't feel like a burden, and one that would clearly point to Him: a cradle and a cross.

After all, the shadow of the cross lay upon Christ even as He rested in the manger.

He came to fulfill the law and the prophets (Matthew 5:17).

He came to preach (Mark 1:38).

He came to do His Father's will (John 6:38).

He came to save the world (John 3:17).

And He came to die (Mark 10:45).

From eternity past, the Father had conceived the plan to rescue from the agony of death every soul who would turn to Him. This rescue required the willing sacrifice of His only Son, the spotless Lamb, nailed to a cross, the place of the great exchange: our sin for His righteousness.

Both the cradle and the cross are inseparable from the gospel.

iv

That month, as I walked and talked with the Lord, I began to dream of what this new display might look like. I imagined a simple wooden cross paired with a small manger. The manger would be filled with carefully wrapped gifts, each one tied with a ribbon and a Bible verse—verses that hinted at what lay inside. As guests visited our home throughout the season, each would be invited to select a gift.

The more I envisioned it, the more I delighted in its purpose: to slow me down, to recenter me, to fix my eyes on Christ, the true reason for the season, and to point others to my Savior. Maybe I would write devotions to go with it, reflections I could revisit year after year. Perhaps each devotion could be paired with a beautiful ornament featuring an illustration on one side and a simple, heartfelt prayer on the other. These would look lovely displayed on the cross.

What should the devotions be about?

> *Therefore, since we have so great a cloud of witnesses surrounding us, let us also lay aside every encumbrance and the sin which so easily entangles us, and let us run with endurance the race that is set before us, fixing our eyes on Jesus, the author and perfecter of faith, who for the joy set before Him endured the cross, despising the shame, and has sat down at the right hand of the throne of God.*
> *—Hebrews 12:1–2*

This powerful passage follows the well-known "hall of faith." The author had just listed name after name from the Old Testament—men and women who put their faith into action. Their lives still speak, echoing through the ages with timeless lessons:

> Give the first and best of all you have to God.
> Obey Him even when no one else does.
> Obey when it seems foolish by the world's standards.
> Keep obeying even when your efforts appear fruitless.
> Trust Him when you don't know where the path leads.
> Believe the impossible.
> Be willing to surrender to Him your greatest treasure.
> Serve Him faithfully until your final breath.

Fear and trust God, not man.
Recall His goodness and encourage others.
Choose nearness to Him over comfort and wealth.
Take Him at His word.
Walk through the doors He opens.
Care for His people.

And the list goes on.

While we don't find a New Testament "hall of faith" laid out in quite the same way, the Gospels are filled with faithful individuals—men and women who encountered Jesus face-to-face. This book will explore snapshots of some of those lives. From the cradle to the cross, they met the Messiah. If we will pause and lay aside distractions, their stories can help us run our race with endurance, keeping our eyes firmly fixed on Christ.

You don't need to have a cradle and a cross, like my Manger to Mercy display, set up in your home to benefit from this little devotional. And just to be clear—I hold zero judgment if you put up a Christmas tree year after year! Though these reflections were born for the Advent season, meant to be read from December 1 to Christmas Day, they can nourish your soul in any season. Truly, there is no wrong way or time to slow down and intentionally fix your eyes on Jesus.

These devotions are short and could be read quickly, but I encourage you not to rush. Take your time. Before opening God's Word, invite the Holy Spirit to open your mind, to reveal hidden treasures. When you reach the "What About You" sections, pause to genuinely reflect. Journal your thoughts, your questions, your prayers.

As you enter into prayer, make it meaningful. Light a candle. Kneel. Open your hands to God as a quiet act of surrender and receptivity.

Many of the songs suggested are not just melodies, but prayers poured out to God—true expressions of worship. As you lift your voice, engage your heart. Ponder the words. Worship in spirit and in truth.

What might we discover as we become intimately acquainted with those who saw Christ face-to-face? How might their lives stir us toward deeper love, stronger faith, and unwavering hope? How might their encounters help replace our doubts with confident trust?

Join me on this journey. Let's find out—together.

Day 1
Mary: Yielded Servant

Read Luke 1:26–38.

The angel Gabriel addressed Mary as "favored one." The God of the universe pursued this young woman with grace and honored her with blessing. Rather than eagerly accepting this greeting, she found it deeply unsettling, troubling. She kept trying to resolve in her mind why this angel would be saying such things to her. Was he the real deal? Were his intentions good and pure, or was this some kind of trap cloaked in light? Did Mary take a moment to consider the cost? In that instant, could she even begin to comprehend what the cost would be?

She voiced her question honestly, "How can this be . . . ?" In response, Gabriel unveiled a mystery—revelation far beyond the scope of her world. It defied logic, stretched her imagination, yet came wrapped with divine assurance. **Mary, in quiet surrender, answered, "Behold, the bondslave of the Lord; may it be done to me according to your word" (v. 38).**

As a result of her quiet submission to that holy conception, what sacred moments would fill her life?
- A spirit that rejoiced and magnified the Lord because she was chosen by Him (Luke 1:46–48).
- Common shepherds proclaiming heaven's glory over her newborn Son (Luke 2:8–19).
- A devout man, eyes clouded with time, speaking profound words about the baby in her arms (Luke 2:25–35).
- Wise men from far-off lands bowing low and bestowing lavish gifts at tiny feet (Matthew 2:11).
- Her adolescent Son drawing near to God and displaying spiritual wisdom beyond His years (Luke 2:46–49).

- Jesus's miracle-working power and glory as she encouraged men to follow His direction (John 2:3–11).
- His extravagant love as He tenderly cared for her even in His suffering (John 19:26–27).

Through rejoicing and through sorrow, from His cradle to His cross, Mary remained close to Jesus. As she heard angels and men from all walks of life proclaiming amazing things about her Boy, she treasured these things in her heart.

What About You?

Does your spirit rejoice, and do you magnify the Lord knowing that you, too, have been chosen by Him? What burdens lay heavy upon you today? Bring them to Jesus. Lay them at His feet and watch His glory meet your need. Let your heart become a sanctuary of truth—cherish every word spoken of Him and the glimpses of grace you discover in His Word. Reflect deeply on the cross of Jesus where His boundless love was poured out for you. Be watchful. God may place someone in Your path today who needs encouragement to heed His words. When you examine yourself, do you see the heart of a servant? How might you willingly yield to His sovereign design for your life?

Pray

Lord, make me more like Mary. How can I not rejoice with all that is in me? You, the Savior of the world, chose me, a frail and lowly sinner. You invite me to cast all my cares at Your feet, and as I do, You rise in strength, moving heaven and earth on my behalf. Draw me into Your Word this Christmas season, and open my eyes and heart to the treasure to be found there. I believe the greatest evidence of Your love for me was proven by Your willingness, even determination, to walk the path to Calvary. Give me an ever-deepening understanding of the exchange that happened there—my shame, my ruin, my sin for Your righteousness. May that truth anchor my soul and ignite my obedience. Help me to be faithful to teach, to guide, and to love those You have placed in my life. **I am Your bondslave; may Your will be done in my life.**

"Sing praises to God, sing praises; Sing praises to our King, sing praises" (Psalm 47:6).

- "Breath of Heaven (Mary's Song)" by Amy Grant (1992)
- "I Will Follow" by Chris Tomlin (2010)
- "Take My Life and Let It Be" by Frances R. Havergal (1874)

Notes

_____

_____

_____

_____

_____

_____

_____

_____

_____

_____

_____

_____

_____

_____

_____

Day 2
John the Baptist: A Life of Humility

Read John 3:25–30.

John the Baptist—what man had a greater cause for pride? From his mother's womb, the Spirit filled his being (Luke 1:15). His name was not a choice of his parents but a declaration from heaven itself (Luke 1:13). At only eight days old, his father's mouth poured forth prophecy: "You, child, . . . will go on before the Lord to prepare His ways" (Luke 1:76). Imagine, having your life's calling etched in ancient prophecies. As the inaugural prophet since Malachi's pen fell silent, he shattered four hundred years of prophetic void. His ministry, so powerful, stirred whispers of Elijah reborn (John 1:21). Even the Lamb of God Himself honored John to be the greatest human ever born (Matthew 11:11). Such a life could swell any heart with pride!

With throngs flocking to hear his message, John could have basked in the light of fame, eaten the fruit of admiration, and adorned himself in robes of honor. Instead, he lived a life of obscurity in the desert. With every reason to declare himself a figure of grand destiny, he chose to lower himself. When Christ came on the scene, he did not cling to the spotlight. **He stepped aside, content to fade, as he humbly declared, "He must increase, but I must decrease" (John 3:30).**

Instead of pride, do we not witness the quiet glory of a humble life as we study John?
- Even as an unborn babe, he leaped with joy at the nearness of Jesus (Luke 1:44).
- He humbly acknowledged Jesus was mightier than he, that he was unworthy even to serve Him, and that Jesus alone had the authority to apportion salvation and judgment (Matthew 3:11–12).

- John recognized Jesus as the holy Son of God and openly made this declaration (John 1:29–34).
- Again and again, he deflected praise and attention, pointing always to the Lamb of God (John 1:35–39).

From infancy through adulthood, John's life was marked by humility. His thoughts, his words, his deeds all magnified Christ, the Lamb of God who takes away the sins of the world.

What About You?

Do you rejoice at the nearness of Jesus—truly rejoice as John did in the womb, stirred by the presence of the Savior? Do you recognize His might, far surpassing your own, and your unworthiness to serve Him? Yet as He called John, so He has called you to walk in His ways, to serve His purposes, to prepare the way for others to know Him. How might you answer that call today? Do you tremble in awe realizing salvation and judgment rest in His hands? No matter your deeds or reputation, do you understand your need for the cleansing that only He can provide? Pause now. Lift your eyes to the holy Son of God and thank Him for the mercy that made a way for your salvation. Even if you have already received the indwelling Holy Spirit, do you embrace your need for His constant, renewing presence? He is not stingy with His Spirit. Ask Him to fill you afresh—He delights to answer that prayer. Today, be ready. Watch for an opportunity to point another to Christ. When praise and recognition come your way, let it pass through your hands and rise to heaven.

Pray

Lord, make me more like John the Baptist. I rejoice at Your nearness—what joy it is to be in the presence of my Savior! You are mighty beyond measure; I am unworthy. Yet You have called me by name and summoned me to Your service. How rich is Your grace that allows me to walk in the good works You have prepared for me. I tremble with holy awe knowing judgment rests in Your hands, yet my heart rests in the peace of Your salvation, freely given. Jesus, Son of God, let me never lose sight of my unending, desperate need for You. Help me to consistently point others to this same truth. Please fill me to overflowing with Your Holy Spirit. **May I decrease and You be magnified in and through my life.**

"Sing praises to God, sing praises; Sing praises to our King, sing praises" (Psalm 47:6).

- "Hark the Herald Angels Sing" by Nat King Cole (1963)
- "Humble" by Audrey Assad (2013)
- "When I Survey the Wondreous Cross" by Isaac Watts (1707)

Notes

_____

_____

_____

_____

_____

_____

_____

_____

_____

_____

_____

_____

_____

_____

Day 3
The Shepherds: Making Christ Famous

Read Luke 2:8–20.

Shepherds—uneducated, overlooked, and often considered unclean by the standards of their day—were the people to receive heaven's birth announcement. Not kings in palaces, not scholars in temples, simply common men. It was there, in the hush of an ordinary night under a canopy of stars, the Light of the World pierced the dark. God, in His wisdom, chose the lowly to witness the holy. He honored these humble men with a divine visit.

When we've tasted the mountaintop, when we've encountered the holy in a way that stirs our soul, don't we long to stay there? We want to hold on to the wonder, to linger in the glory. But these shepherds didn't stay in the fields. Beholding God's fulfilled promise compelled them to joyfully carry the extraordinary into the ordinary. **We read, "When they had seen this, they made known the statement which had been told them about this Child. And all who heard it wondered at the things which were told them by the shepherds" (vv. 17–18).**

How did the shepherds respond when they heard heaven's good news and beheld this precious Baby?
- "Let us . . ." The glory of God ignited not only wonder but unity. These men, bound by a shared awe, rose together with one purpose: to seek and behold the newborn King.
- When the glory of God lit up the dark night these lowly men labored under, they left behind their flocks and made haste to pursue the Great Shepherd. They had heard about Him; now they wanted to encounter Him.
- Though they may not have grasped the full weight of prophecy or the depth of the mystery before them, their hearts overflowed. What they

knew, they shared with joy—the good news entrusted to them was too precious to keep to themselves.

- When the moment passed, they did not return the same. Back to their fields they went, but with hearts transformed, praising and glorifying God and carrying eternal joy into their everyday labor.

Surely it was no accident that God chose to first reveal His Son to shepherds. Centuries before, the prophet Micah declared that the Messiah would "shepherd His flock" (Micah 5:4). Jesus would later call Himself the "door of the sheep" (John 10:7). A few verses later He names Himself the "good shepherd" (John 10:11). Peter calls our Savior the "Chief Shepherd" (1 Peter 5:4). As God always does, He seemed to be communicating layers of truth as He unfolded His sovereign plan.

What About You?

Do you recognize the treasure you hold in your hands—the living, breathing Word of God? Though the world may count you foolish, weak, lowly, or even despised, do you understand that such are the hearts God delights to fill with His light (1 Corinthians 1:27–28)? Are you walking with others who seek Him? Are you part of a fellowship where God is encountered, worshipped, and made known through shared mission and faith? If not, ask God where and with whom He wants you to grow. How will you intentionally pursue Christ today? Do you hesitate to share anything because you don't know everything? Don't let that hinder you! You don't need every answer to speak of what you've seen and heard. Recognize Jesus's presence in the midst of your daily toil, and experience the joy to be found there.

Pray

Lord, make me more like the shepherds. Though I am small and undeserving, You, the King of the universe, have chosen to bring Your good news to me. What grace! What mercy! My heart overflows with gratitude. Please deepen my friendships with Your people and knit our hearts together. May our collective pursuit lead us to exalt You, celebrate You, and magnify You in our everyday lives. As I move through the rhythms of daily life, help me to sense Your nearness. Let Your presence turn the mundane into sacred ground, infusing my journey with joy. On this side of heaven, I know I will never fully grasp the depths of who You are and all You have done, but give me courage to share what You are teaching me. Lord, You disclose so many wonderful things to me through Your Word. **Let my lips and my life make You famous.**

"Sing praises to God, sing praises; Sing praises to our King, sing praises" (Psalm 47:6).

- "Go Tell it on the Mountains" by Maverick City Music (2021)
- "My Jesus" by Anne Wilson (2022)
- "I Love to Tell the Story" by Katherine Hankey (1866)

Notes

_____

_____

_____

_____

_____

_____

_____

_____

_____

_____

_____

_____

_____

_____

Day 4
The Magi: Extravagant Worship

Read Matthew 2:1–12.

Matthew offers only glimpses of these mysterious travelers. Scholars puzzle over their story—where exactly they came from, how many followed the star, precisely when they arrived, where Jesus was when they visited. One thing is undeniable: They came with hearts ready to worship. The precious gifts they carried seem to have significance. Gold was the treasure of kings (1 Kings 10:21). Frankincense was a key ingredient in the sacred incense used for worship in the tabernacle and the temple, and God instructed that the bread of the Presence be covered with this valuable resin (Leviticus 24:7). Myrrh was a spice used in Jewish burial rites (John 19:39–40).

These men embarked on a long and arduous journey, possibly up to nine hundred miles, with no certainty of their destination. Can you imagine doing the same? What exactly did they believe about Jesus that made Him worth such a sacrifice? God greatly rewarded their willingness to seek Him with all their hearts, for we discover the pinnacle of their journey: **After coming into the house, they saw the Child with Mary His mother, and they fell to the ground and worshipped Him (Matthew 2:11).**

What does Scripture reveal about the magi?
- They were students of ancient prophecies, familiar with the sacred words that whispered about a coming Messiah and therefore able to discern when and where to begin searching for Jesus.
- They "rejoiced exceedingly with great joy," the sort of joy that springs from faith, when they saw the star they anticipated would lead them to the King of the Jews.
- Jesus had not yet spoken with authority. He had not yet healed a single

sick person. He had cast out no demons. He had done nothing that would inspire worship, yet these men fell to the ground and worshipped Him because of who they believed Him to be.

- With the gifts of their worship, the magi seemed to speak without words: gold for the King they had come to honor, frankincense for the divine presence they sensed in the Child, myrrh for the mortal sorrow that awaited Him.

Their story reminds us that true worship begins not with proof but with faith and that those who earnestly seek God will find Him, just as He promised.

What About You?
What might you lay down today in pursuit of Jesus? What comforts, distractions, or routines might you surrender in order to draw nearer to the One who left heaven to seek you first? Determine to set aside some time to linger in His Word, the sacred place He makes Himself known. Allow Scripture to fan the flames of your faith and ask Him how He would have you respond. As Jesus, the Light of the World, reveals Himself to you, let your heart be filled with joy not tied to circumstances but rooted in relationship. Devote some time to worship Jesus for who He is—the King of Kings, the divine gift of deity wrapped in fragile flesh, born to die that you might live. Consider how you might lavish extravagant worship upon Him today.

Pray
Lord, make me more like the magi. Stir within me a desire to unearth treasure in Your Word, treasure far more precious than gold and silver. Tune my ear to the wisdom in Your pages, and incline my heart to the knowledge that waits to be discovered. Open my eyes to Your glory being declared by the heavens. As You reveal Yourself to me, grow my affection for You and cause my life to overflow with the joy that comes from life lived in Your presence. Jesus, You are my King, an indescribably marvelous gift, my Savior. **I worship You with open hands, freely offering every good thing You have given that all may be used for Your kingdom and Your glory alone.**

"Sing praises to God, sing praises; Sing praises to our King, sing praises" (Psalm 47:6).

- "Little Drummer Boy" by Pentatonix (2013)
- "Here I am to Worship" by Chris Tomlin (2002)
- "God Himself is With Us" by Gerhardt Tersteegen (1729)

Notes

_____

_____

_____

_____

_____

_____

_____

_____

_____

_____

_____

_____

_____

_____

_____

Day 5
Peter: A Life Refined

Read John 21:15–22.

Often our greatest strengths can become our undoing if left untamed. So it is with Peter—a young man ablaze with ability, fierce in devotion, quick to act and speak. Before Jesus laid hold of his heart, he was as wild and unpredictable as the seas he once fished. When Jesus began to reveal the path of salvation that would come through His suffering, death, and resurrection, Peter took Him aside and rebuked Him. Peter rebuked the Lord! Jesus loved him too much to leave him misguided and had his own strong rebuke for Peter: "Get behind Me, Satan! You are a stumbling block to Me; for you are not setting your mind on God's interests, but man's" (Matthew 16:23).

This rhythm of impetuous strength and gracious refinement plays out again and again in Peter's story. When Jesus knelt to wash His disciples' feet, Peter recoiled, declaring, "Never shall You wash my feet!" (John 13:8). When Jesus foretold that all would fall away, Peter's loyalty flared like wildfire: "Even though all may fall away because of You, I will never fall away" (Matthew 26:33). But Jesus, with tender foresight, spoke plainly, "Before a rooster crows, you will deny Me three times" (Matthew 26:34). You likely know how the story unfolds. A courtyard. A fire. A servant girl's question. Three denials. Bitter tears. Just as Jesus had said. But Peter did not flee forever into shame. He did not let failure define him. **Peter received the discipline of the Lord and allowed Love to refine him.**

How do we witness Peter's life refined by the Lord?
* The incident of Peter's rebuke. The Lord's sharp words must have pierced more than just Peter's pride. Scripture doesn't record Peter's response, but we do read that six days later Peter was still walking with the Rabbi

who had rebuked him. Still following. Still listening (Matthew 17:1). Perhaps he carried the sting of shame for a moment, but he chose presence over distance, humility over retreat.

- The foot-washing episode. Peter did one of his famous pendulum swings here. As Jesus knelt to wash His feet, Peter resisted. Then he swung from refusal to overcorrection, "Lord, then wash not only my feet, but also my hands and my head" (John 13:9). Jesus gently redirected him, and Peter—fervent, still learning—yielded. He heard the words of his Teacher, understood the meaning, and bowed to wisdom greater than his own.

- The denial and restoration. Surely, for days and nights to come, the crowing of a rooster became a cruel reminder of Peter's greatest failure. But Jesus would not let the story end in sorrow. At daybreak, on a shore glistening with new light, the Savior asked Peter not once but three times, "Do you love Me?" (John 21:15–17). Three denials, now met with three opportunities to declare his love. Restoration echoed over regret. And perhaps, just as Peter spoke the third affirmation, a rooster crowed in the distance—not to condemn but to remind him: Mercy had the final word.

Peter was part of Jesus's inner circle. For years, I assumed this was because he was the cream of the crop, until a wise pastor pointed out that teachers often keep trouble-prone students at the front of the class. Discipline is difficult. It humbles. It stings. It exposes our faults—sometimes in full view of others. Peter allowed correction to chisel him.

What About You?
Do you have a wise brother or sister investing in you, one who lovingly reveals the blind spots you cannot see, who speaks the truth in love, who helps you discern when your heart is set on human concerns instead of God's eternal purposes? If not, ask God who you might invite into this role. When the Lord's discipline comes, don't shrink away. Remember: He disciplines those He loves, shaping us for our good, so that we may share His holiness, and so that it "yields the peaceful fruit of righteousness" (Hebrews 12:6–11). Draw near, learn, and be transformed. Train your ears to listen to the Lord, gain understanding from His words, and commit to submit to His will. How has the Lord tenderly lifted you when you have stumbled? Hold that memory close today and rest in His love for you.

Pray

Lord, make me more like Peter. Give me courage to seek accountability, trusting You to use a brother or sister to help mold my heart and life. Though discipline never feels pleasant, I know You to be a good Father, and I have seen Your hand bring beauty from correction. May I never flee from You in shame or embarrassment but always rest in the depth of Your unfailing love. Grant me the fortitude to lean in close to You. Give me ears eager to hear Your voice, a mind hungry for understanding, and a heart willing to follow You no matter the cost. **I choose to yield to Your loving and merciful discipline; refine me as silver.**

"Sing praises to God, sing praises; Sing praises to our King, sing praises" (Psalm 47:6).

- "The Christ The King" by Bryanand Katie Torwalt (2022)
- "Canvas and Clay" by Pat Barrett (2019)
- "Sanctuary" by John Thomas and Randy Scruggs (1982)

Notes

_____

_____

_____

_____

_____

_____

_____

_____

_____

_____

Day 6
Nicodemus: A Journey of Discovery

Read John 3:1–17.

Nicodemus was no ordinary man—he was a Pharisee of stature, a respected leader among those whose hearts grew increasingly hostile toward Jesus, the One who defied their endless rules and unyielding traditions. Bound by timidity and the fear of man, Nicodemus chose the cover of darkness for his first encounter with Jesus, slipping through the night to meet the Light. What would his peers say if they knew he sought the company of the One drawing crowds and stirring hearts?

Jesus, ever gracious, met him there in the quiet of night and welcomed the honest questions of a cautious soul. Their conversation was unguarded and deep, though Nicodemus seemed to leave with more mystery than clarity. Still, something had been planted. Scripture offers only glimpses of him, but each time he emerges, he seems changed—more aware, more courageous. **The man who once crept by night later stepped into the light of day, bearing spices and reverence, tending to the broken body of the crucified Christ.**

How do we see Nicodemus's journey from timid inquiry to bold allegiance?
- In the first encounter we read about between Nicodemus and Jesus, it seems Nicodemus was ashamed at the thought of being seen with Jesus. Though Jesus has challenging words for those who are ashamed of or deny Him (Luke 9:26; Matthew 10:33), He does not condemn Nicodemus. Jesus meets him with patience, not expecting instant perfection, and gently guides him toward truth.
- In Nicodemus's second appearance in Scripture, timidity begins to give way to boldness. Before the powerful members of the Jewish high court, he raises his voice in defense of Jesus, challenging the injustice of His

condemnation (John 7:50–52).

- Finally, we find Nicodemus at the foot of the cross. As others scatter in fear, he steps into the open. On the eve of a high Sabbath during Passover, Nicodemus chooses reverence over ritual, love over legalism. In caring for Jesus's lifeless body, he knowingly makes himself ceremonially unclean (John 19:38–42).

Even the most devout and outwardly righteous person stands in need of the new birth that only Jesus can give. For some, that faith is implanted in an instant, sudden and sure; for others, like Nicodemus, the path toward belief unfolds more gradually, winding through searching questions and quiet reflection.

What About You?

Is there a circle where you feel a sense of belonging yet speaking the name of Jesus would cost you comfort or approval? Does the fear of man ever ring louder in your ears than the fear of God in your heart? If so, remember you are not alone and you are not condemned; however, Jesus does not want you to remain in a place of shame over or denial of belonging to Him. Ask Him to replace any apprehension with boldness to speak about Him. Spend time with Him in His Word and prayer and invite the Holy Spirit to awaken your understanding. Today, how might you live so that those around you cannot help but recognize where your allegiance lies—with Christ, your Savior and King?

Pray

Lord, make me more like Nicodemus. I confess there have been times when fear has held me back, when I hesitated to declare or display my allegiance to You. I am thankful that You meet my weakness not with condemnation but with compassion. You gently guide me toward growth and maturity. Please increase my faith. As I meditate on the truth of Your Word, open my mind to understanding and my heart to trust. I know you have not given me a spirit of timidity. Grow boldness in me—a courage rooted not in confidence in myself but in confidence in You. At Christmas parties and family gatherings, in shopping lines and conversations with strangers, let me speak of Your love and truth without shrinking back, no matter who is listening. **Though at times my faith has lingered in the shadows, give me a chance today to raise my voice and publicly proclaim my love and devotion to You.**

"Sing praises to God, sing praises; Sing praises to our King, sing praises" (Psalm 47:6).

- "Silent Night" by Jewel (1999)
- "Through it All" by Colton Dixon (2014)
- "I'm Not Ashamed to Own the Lord" by Isaac Watts (1707)

Notes

_____

_____

_____

_____

_____

_____

_____

_____

_____

_____

_____

_____

_____

_____

Day 1
The Woman of Samaria: Fully Known

Read John 4:3–29, 39.

This unnamed woman first happens upon Jesus in His human frailty, wearied from traveling, resting beside a well. Little did she suspect in that ordinary moment that she stood face-to-face with the gift of God. Recognizing Him as a Jew, she was taken aback by the kindness He extended, so unlike the disdain she had come to expect. With her eyes focused on temporal things, she saw only a tired man with a bucket. She judged Him by what He lacked, unable to fathom the power He held or the overflowing satisfaction He had to offer.

This woman did not recoil or lash out, as many might if a stranger uncovered their sinful ways. Instead, she received His gentle reproof with grace, acknowledging this stranger as a prophet who somehow knew the secrets she carried. Sensing He had some connection to God, she leaned in rather than turning away, her heart stirred to learn from Him. She did not yet fully grasp who Jesus was, but she began to realize something remarkable: He knew her. Truly knew her. **And in her own words, she would later testify with wonder, "He told me all the things that I have done" (v. 29).**

What did Christ know about this woman?
- He knew her heart even before she spoke. He knew that if she had recognized Him for who He truly was, she would not have responded with curt skepticism, but would have drawn near, thirsting for what He had to offer.
- He knew her immorality. He laid the weight of her sin upon her gently, not crushing her with condemnation. Instead, He pierced her heart with truth, that she might long to lay that yolk upon Him and taste the healing only He could bring.

26

- He knew the confusion that clouded her understanding of worship. In centuries past, her people had been taught to worship the Lord, but they continued to make idols and worship false gods. "They feared the LORD and served their own gods" (2 Kings 17:33).

Jesus points out her ignorance and her immorality, things we typically seek to conceal from onlookers. To be fully known, yet neither condemned nor shamed, stirred within this woman a longing she may never have realized was there. This deep, tender intimacy with Christ was unlike anything she had experienced before in her life. It was a moment so transformative that she abandoned her water pot, her earthly concerns, and returned home to tell her neighbors about her unexpected meeting with the suspected Messiah.

What About You?

Many recognize Jesus as a good man, different from others, yet miss the truth that He is the gift of God. Having read this far, you have likely already unwrapped the gift of eternal life found in Christ, but have you tasted the fullness of satisfaction found in His presence? Do you draw daily from the river of His delights? In Him there is a deep well of fulfillment that can be found nowhere else. Baring your soul before another can be intimidating. What will they think of me if they know who I really am? Jesus already knows the deepest recesses of your heart—all the beauty and all the brokenness. And still He loves you completely. Lean in and bask in the warmth of this most intimate relationship. Then ask yourself who might need to know such love. Whose heart could be refreshed by the abundance you've found?

Pray

Lord, make me more like the woman of Samaria. May I never shrink away when you shine light on my sin. She stood before You unaware of who You truly were, but I know You now: the gift of God, the Savior who bore my shame and paid my debt in full. Thank you that there is no condemnation for me. Let Your living water fill me to overflowing. Make me purposeful in this season that so often rushes by to slow down and find joy and gladness in Your presence. Satisfy my soul and open my mouth to praise You. Explore the hidden places of my heart, Lord. Reveal what's anxious, what's broken, what's misaligned with Your goodness. If anything within me strays from Your way, gently lead me back to what is true and eternal. **I rejoice to be fully known and perfectly loved by You!**

"Sing praises to God, sing praises; Sing praises to our King, sing praises" (Psalm 47:6).

- "O Holy Night" by Kerrie Roberts (2011)
- "Hungry (Falling on My Knees)" by Kathryn Scott (1999)
- "I Heard the Voice of Jesus Say" by Horatius Bonar (1846)

Notes

_____

_____

_____

_____

_____

_____

_____

_____

_____

_____

_____

_____

_____

_____

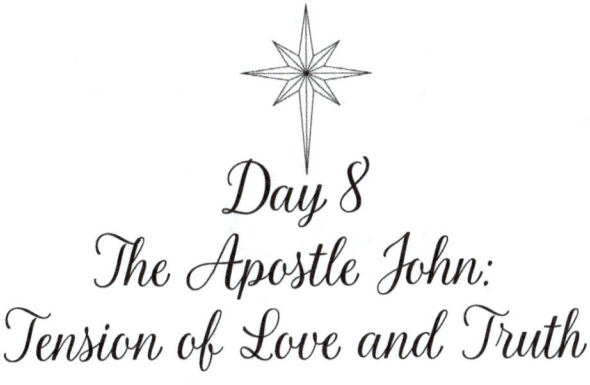

Day 8
The Apostle John:
Tension of Love and Truth

Read 1 John 2:4–11.

Warren Wiersbe once observed, "Truth without love is brutality, and love without truth is hypocrisy." John certainly did not struggle with hypocrisy in his early days of ministry! Jesus didn't call John a "son of thunder" without reason (Mark 3:17). John, along with others, once tried to prevent someone from delivering people who were suffering from demons because the person was not part of their inner circle (Luke 9:49). Not long after, John suggested calling down fire from heaven to consume a village that refused to welcome Jesus (Luke 9:53–54). Jesus was not impressed either time!

John spoke with conviction, never mincing words regarding those who failed to live the truth they professed (1 John 1:6; 2:4). For him, truth was not merely a doctrine to defend but a path to walk. His greatest joy was cultivating truth in the hearts of others and witnessing them walk in that truth (3 John 1:4). A passion for truth seemed to be wired into John's DNA, to pulse through his very being. Yet as the years unfolded and he walked more closely with Jesus, we begin to see that zeal for truth tempered with love for people. **John reached the maturity spoken of in Ephesians 4:15: "But speaking the truth in love, we are to grow up in all aspects into Him who is the head, even Christ."**

How do we eventually witness John beautifully balancing love and truth?
- We find a tender glimpse at the cross, where Jesus entrusts the care of His own mother to John (John 19:25–27). Certainly, Christ would not have placed such a sacred responsibility in the hands of a harsh, immature man.

- Later, in his letters, John speaks with the warmth of a spiritual father: "Little children, let us not love in word or with tongue, but in deed and truth" (1 John 3:18). As they should be, love and truth became inseparable for John.
- John opens two of his epistles declaring his love in truth for the recipients (2 John 1:1; 3 John 1:1). John had come to understand that true love does not lash out in anger, nor does it wander outside the boundaries of God's commands (1 John 5:2).

Imagine a tug-of-war, with truth on one end and love on the other. In today's culture—and sometimes even in the church—the pull often favors love. But in Scripture, love and truth aren't rivals. They stand firm together, each holding their place. John learned to hold these two virtues in perfect tension.

What About You?

Does your heart's pendulum swing too far in one direction? Perhaps your zeal for truth rushes ahead, leaving behind a trail of hasty judgments and harsh words. Or maybe your deep compassion holds you back from speaking hard truths—fearing discomfort, even when those very words could guide someone closer to Christ. Whichever might describe you, are you taking steps to grow into maturity, to balance these two qualities? Look to Jesus. Look to John. Look to other pillars of the faith who held love and truth in harmony. Hide God's words in your heart that will help you live this balance well. Christ may not be appointing you to care for His mother, but He does ask you to love the people around you. Who can you intentionally love in truth today?

Pray

Lord, make me more like John. Help me to be steadfast in love and unwavering in truth. Forgive me for the times I have spoken the truth cruelly and for the moments I remained silent, mistaking silence for love when I should have spoken up for their good and Your glory. Teach me to walk in love and truth. May I never let go of one to hold the other. This Christmas season, as the world remembers the arrival of Your Son—full of grace and truth—let that same Spirit come alive in me. Give me an opportunity to show someone this kind of love today: bold, compassionate, anchored in truth. Open my eyes to examples of men and women in Scripture who walked this narrow path well and guide me to follow in their footsteps. **Grow me, mature**

me, and help me to reflect the heart of Christ, holding love and truth in perfect balance.

"Sing praises to God, sing praises; Sing praises to our King, sing praises" (Psalm 47:6).

- "Joy to the Word" by JJ Heller (2022)
- "By Our Love" by Christy Nockels (2009)
- "Turn Your Eyes Upon Jesus" by Helen Howarth Lemmel (1918)

Notes

_____

_____

_____

_____

_____

_____

_____

_____

_____

_____

_____

_____

_____

_____

Day 9
The Man from Gerasenes:
A Life Liberated

Read Luke 8:26–39.

Demon possessed. Naked. Living in a graveyard. Seized. Bound. Chained. Isolated. In other Gospels we hear him screaming day and night, a soul in torment. He tore at his own flesh with jagged stones. Luke tells us this was no passing affliction; he had been like this for a long time. Certainly, any flicker of hope had been extinguished long ago. Can you imagine such an existence? Maybe you don't have to; perhaps your life is marked by some sort of bondage.

But then, Jesus. At His feet. Dressed. In his right mind. Whole. The man from Gerasenes, once a burden to his neighbors, his voice a terror in the dark, his presence a menace, was now given a new purpose to carry the mercy of God back to the very people who had once feared him. He who had lived a tormented, lonely life now longed only to be near his Healer. He begged to go with Jesus. **In the flesh we may be tempted to regard Jesus's "no" as rejection, but through eyes of faith we clearly see Jesus had a mission and purpose for this liberated man.**

In what ways did the truth set this man free?
- After one unexpected meeting with the Anointed One, the man once broken and bound was whole and healed. The chains that once clung to both body and soul had fallen.
- He who wandered naked and nameless was now clothed in garments and dignity. Jesus freed him from the ache of isolation, replacing it with the gift of community.
- This man once marked by rage and self-harm bore little resemblance

to the image of God he had been crafted to reflect. In the presence of Christ, the shattered bits of his humanity were restored.
- Once an unwilling instrument of darkness, he was now a living, breathing testimony of the healing, saving power of Jesus.

True freedom is found not in casting off all restraint but in surrendering to righteousness. Abundant life sometimes means sitting at the feet of Jesus—worshipping, learning, being healed. Other times it means self-denial and sacrificial love. Always it means walking in obedience to our Savior.

What About You?
Are you living in bondage to the world, your flesh, or the enemy of your soul? Pause and invite the Lord to search your heart. Are there places in your life that still resist His gentle rule? Are you harming your body, the temple of God's Spirit, in any way? Ask what steps you can take to honor and nurture it instead. God has created you for community. If you find yourself isolated, ask Him what you can do to begin mending broken relationships. Do you carry the weight of shame or brokenness? Are you being manipulated by Satan in any way? Do his lies whisper hopelessness to your soul? Remember: One encounter with Jesus can change everything. He is sovereign over your soul and your story. Turn to him. When the weight is too heavy to bear alone, lean on His church. You were never meant to carry it alone.

Pray
Lord, make me more like the man from Gerasenes. Please show me the places in my life I am enslaved, and break every ungodly influence that keeps me bound. Free me from the grip of sin and Satan and make me a slave to righteousness, for I know Your yoke is easy and Your burden is light. Give me courage and guide me in seeking help from other believers who can come alongside me and help me to walk in the freedom You offer. Teach me to care for my body, Your temple, with wisdom and intention, honoring it as the dwelling place for Your Spirit. Please restore my hope in You and Your power to transform my life. Where I feel lonely, draw me into deeper fellowship with You and into meaningful connection with Your people. Where shame still lingers, cover me with humble confidence in the identity You have given me. Make me look more and more like You, Jesus. Give me opportunities to speak of Your goodness and declare all the wonders You have done in my life. **Set me free me to walk boldly in Your mission and**

purpose for my life.

"Sing praises to God, sing praises; Sing praises to our King, sing praises" (Psalm 47:6).

- "O Come Emmanuel" by Tommee Profitt (2020)
- "I Don't Wanna Go" by Chris Renzema (2018)
- "Power in the Blood" by Lewis E. Jones (1899)

Notes

_____

_____

_____

_____

_____

_____

_____

_____

_____

_____

_____

_____

_____

_____

Day 10
The Hemorrhaging Woman: Determined Faith

Read Mark 5:25–34.

The many hands that were meant to heal only caused her more harm. She endured—in Greek, meaning to suffer, undergo evils, be afflicted—much at their hands. She spent twelve long years and every last resource she had seeking the healing they offered but only became worse in their care. She must have been weak from so many years of shedding blood. Declared unclean and cut off from society, she lived in isolation. Desperate for help, she clung to fragile hope that she could be made well.

Then she heard about Jesus. Faith comes by hearing. She "thought" to herself. The Greek verb here is richer than a passing thought. It means "speak" and is in the imperfect tense, which implies ongoing action: She kept saying to herself. This wasn't a fleeting idea—it was a persistent, inward confession. She was preaching to her own soul. Her inner dialogue could easily have echoed her years of suffering: I will never be well. No one can help me. God has forgotten me. But instead, faith arose, and she spoke truth to herself: This Man can help me; He can make me well. She acted upon this faith deliberately. Purposefully. Courageously. The end of her rope was the fringe of Jesus's cloak. **Many in the crowd touched Jesus that day, but she touched Him with determined faith.**

What came of this quiet faith that was known by the omniscient One?
- The incurable was cured. In an instant Jesus healed this woman who "could not be healed by anyone" (Luke 8:43).
- In fear and trembling she fell before Him in humility. As it is written in Isaiah 66:2, "To this one I will look, to him who is humble and contrite

of spirit, and who trembles at My word."

- Truth led to testimony. Her confession to Christ was overheard by the crowd. Surely her words brought glory to God and encouraged all who heard that suffering isn't the end of the story—healing is possible.
- Her faith led to a divine encounter. Jesus knew the difference between casual contact and the touch of faith. He commended and encouraged her.

When Jesus met this woman, He was on an important and time-sensitive mission. Yet He stopped for her. He acknowledged her. He called her "Daughter."

What About You?

Is there a place in your life where hope has grown dim? Do you find yourself weary, worn by battles you didn't choose, isolated by pain, or stripped of strength and resources? Have you been wounded by hands that were meant to help and heal? Fix your eyes on Jesus. Forge a path toward Him. Cling fiercely to hope. Let persistent prayers rise like incense before His throne. Reach out with determined faith, believing He still works wonders in the wilderness. Bow before Him in reverence, humbly bringing your request. Immerse yourself in His Word and wait expectantly for His answer.

Pray

Lord, make me more like the hemorrhaging woman. Though all reason shouts to give up hope, help me to cling to You, my unshakable hope. I know nothing is impossible for You. Though I am weary, I will not lose heart. Help me to forgive those who have wounded me. Keep my gaze fixed on You. Remove every obstacle and stumbling block that impedes my path to You. I come to You now in fear and trembling, yet drawn by grace. May my prayers be counted as incense before You. I wait for You, and in Your Word, I anchor my hope. This Christmas, as I remember that You came near, I am reminded that You still come close to the desperate and broken-hearted. I will speak of Your wonders. I long for the intimacy found only in Your presence. **So now, in desperate, deliberate, determined faith, I reach out to You, the One who is able and faithful.**

"Sing praises to God, sing praises; Sing praises to our King, sing praises" (Psalm 47:6).

- "Prince of Peace" by Cross Point Music (2021)
- "Worth it All" by Rita Springer (2002)
- "Just as I Am" by Charles Elliot (1835)

Notes

_____

_____

_____

_____

_____

_____

_____

_____

_____

_____

_____

_____

_____

_____

_____

41

Day 11
Matthew: Sinner Turned Saint

Read Luke 5:27–32.

We know little about Matthew—also called Levi—from his days as a sinner other than his profession: tax collector. In ancient Israel, it was regarded one of the most corrupt and abhorred professions. Tax collectors were notorious for inflating dues, fattening their pockets with the surplus, and cheating their way into riches. It was a life of deception, isolation, and fraudulent wealth. No wonder they were despised. Seeing Matthew rise without hesitation to Jesus's call, we have to wonder if his heart was weary with the weight of such a life.

When Matthew left "everything" behind to follow Jesus, that included the ledgers, the coins, and the path he had walked, yet he did not abandon the people who had walked that path with him. The very next scene finds Matthew hosting a feast in Jesus's honor. His table was filled with others like himself—tax collectors and outcasts still far from God. It is a powerful image: a man newly called, not retreating from the world but inviting it to sit at the feet of grace. His story reminds us that Christ calls us not only to walk away from darkness but to invite others to the Light. **Matthew's calling magnifies the abundant grace of God.**

What did Matthew's new life as a saint look like?
- He didn't waste time to tidy his soul or attempt to earn righteousness before following Christ. In the very midst of a profession marked by greed and deception, he heard the call and rose. No bargaining. No delay. Just a heart that somehow knew holiness was not earned but offered.
- He walked away from a life of comfort and certainty where wealth had secured his days. In its place, he chose the dusty roads of discipleship to

follow a Rabbi who had no home.

- He gathered his fellow sinners and invited them to sit near the guest of honor. Unashamed, he turned his table into a mission field.
- In time, this once-despised tax collector would pen a Gospel so rich with the words and works of Christ that it would become the second most beloved books in all of Scripture.[1]

According to Jesus's own words, if you are not a sinner, He didn't come for you. By calling Matthew, Jesus is declaring that no one is beyond the reach of grace, even those the world calls the worst.

What About You?

Do you recognize your sinfulness? Does it prevent you from drawing near to Jesus? Please don't let that be the case! That brokenness is exactly the reason you need to lean in closer. Who do you surround yourself with? Of course, it is wise to walk closely with a fellowship of people rooted in faith, but do you still brush shoulders with the lost, those shackled with sin and desperate for the hope you carry? Is there a friend you've drifted away from because they don't share your faith? Perhaps now is the time to reach out. A simple invitation to coffee or lunch may open the door to God's Word, gently, in time. Are there pieces of your old life that you still cling to? Habits, comforts, distractions that no longer belong? Ask Him for the grace to let go, and use the freed-up time to pursue the harvest He has appointed you to gather.

Pray

Lord, make me more like Matthew. Give me courage to lay aside every encumbrance and the sin that so easily entangles me so that I can run hard after You. I bring before You my brokenness, my failings, my sin. Thank You for taking that upon Yourself and clothing me in Your righteousness. Because of Your mercy, I now come with confidence, drawing near without fear. As I walk through this season, when the world remembers how mercy came wrapped in flesh, may I not miss the call to follow You with wholehearted devotion. Is there someone in my world who needs a glimpse of Your love? Bring them to mind. Inspire me in what way I might

---

1 J. Peterson, *The 10 Most Popular Bible Books*, Bible Gateway, April 21, 2014, https://www.biblegateway.com/blog/2014/04/the-10-most-popular-books-of-the-bible-and-why/.

bless them. I know You have good plans for my gifts and my time. Please guide me along that path today. **Allow my life to reflect Your mercy and to magnify Your grace.**

"Sing praises to God, sing praises; Sing praises to our King, sing praises" (Psalm 47:6).

- "Light of the World (Sing Hallelujah)" by We the Kingdom (2021)
- "Redeemed" by Big Daddy Weave (2012)
- "Amazing Grace" by John Newton (1779)

Notes

_____

_____

_____

_____

_____

_____

_____

_____

_____

_____

_____

_____

45

Day 12
The Woman Who Loved Much: Genuine Repentance

Read Luke 7:36–50.

Like everyone else, Jesus was fully aware of the weight and breadth of this woman's sins. Nothing was hidden from Him—every failure, every shameful act, every wound she had both inflicted and endured. While Simon looked upon her with judgment and disdain, measuring her worth by her past, Jesus looked deeper, saw her faith, and had already fully forgiven her. The words "have been forgiven" in verses 47 and 48 of this passage are translated from a single Greek word, *aphiémi*, that reveals a beautiful truth: her sins were already forgiven at some point prior to this sacred encounter. She did not come to earn forgiveness that night; she came because she had already received it.

Surely, she had heard His voice before: His call to the weary, the broken, the burdened, to come and find rest. Oh, how her life must have been full of despair and distress before she met Him! His message—life for those who believe—must have silenced the storm raging in her soul. Jesus publicly affirmed what had already taken place in the quiet of her heart. How sweetly His words must have rung in her ears, "Your faith has saved you; go in peace" (v. 50). **By grace, through her genuine repentance and faith, her soul found stillness in the voice of the One who forgives and frees.**

In what ways does this woman's love and devotion for Jesus burn bright against the cold backdrop of Simon's self-righteousness?
- No kiss of greeting and acceptance, no water to refresh weary feet, no oil to anoint the honored guest. Simon neglected even the most basic acts of hospitality; she offered all she had. The very instruments of her

former life—her hair, her perfume, her lips—once used for seduction, now vessels of sacred adoration.

- Tears that once traced the path of shame in secret now flowed freely before all. In this instance, they poured forth as a public display of her sorrow over sin and true repentance. Simon, smugly rejecting the beauty of her brokenness, could only sneer and remember who she once had been.

- As she broke open her costly perfume, the fragrance of her sacrifice and repentance filled the house. Her actions testified to Jesus's worth in a language Simon couldn't understand. While her devotion declared Him worthy of all, Simon sat silent, revealing a stingy heart unmoved by the presence of God.

Each of us bears a debt we cannot repay. Do we grasp its weight or our inability to clear it? Do we recognize the boundless grace of our Savior who paid it in full, rescuing us from a disaster worse than death?

What About You?

Have you turned to Jesus in genuine repentance? Or does some hidden sin still weigh heavily upon your soul? The Lord stands ready to lift that burden from you if you will turn to Him. Believe His promise: If you come to Him, He will give you rest. He will lead you beside quiet waters. He will restore your soul. Cease striving to pay your debt—it is impossible. Instead, allow Jesus's forgiveness to wash over you until tears of shame and regret are transformed into tears of godly sorrow. Worship the One who purchased your pardon. How might you offer your body as a living sacrifice today? In what tangible way can love and thankfulness shape your response to His mercy?

Pray

Lord, make me more like the woman who loved much. Let her grateful heart become my own, always remembering that You canceled the record of my debt, nailing it to the cross. Keep me from the subtle pride of comparing my sins to another's, as if mine could be deemed less offensive. Jesus, You are so worthy of all my gratitude, praise, and worship. Untangle me from anything that clings to me and clouds my vision. I long to see You more clearly, love You more deeply, and offer myself more fully. May the fragrance of Christ emanate from my life, drawing men, woman, and children to You. **Thank You that when I turn to You in repentance and faith, You faithfully wash**

47

away the guilt of my sins, inviting me to live a life full of peace and joy in Your presence.

"Sing praises to God, sing praises; Sing praises to our King, sing praises" (Psalm 47:6).

- "God with Us" by All Sons & Daughters (2014)
- "Knees to the Earth" by Watermark (2004)
- "My Jesus, I Love Thee" by William Ralph Featherston (1862)

Notes

_____

_____

_____

_____

_____

_____

_____

_____

_____

_____

_____

_____

_____

_____

Day 13
A Canaanite Woman: Unshakable Faith

Read Matthew 15:21–28.

Most of us can find ourselves in the story of this woman. We, too, have cried out and had our prayers met with silence. We have pleaded fervently for a child, a friend, or a spouse under the influence of Satan, only to watch as heaven seemed to withhold the answer we desperately hoped for. We have been dealt a divine "no" when we were sure our own will was aligned with the Word and will of God. In those moments, how tempting it is to lose hope and believe God is distant, indifferent, or even unjust. When affliction comes, our hearts naturally crave relief. We want it gone swiftly and completely, convinced that deliverance must be what is best. However, Jesus sees through time and beyond circumstance and knows what is truly good. There are advantages to waiting for His answer.

The Lord knew the strength of this woman's faith and that she would stand the test of His silence, His refusal, His seemingly harsh evaluation of her. Her perseverance was no accident; it was the proving ground of genuine trust. Scripture tells us the proof, the tested genuineness, of our faith is more precious than gold (1 Peter 1:7). **Jesus was drawing out a trustworthy faith in this woman as He gave her the opportunity to persist in prayer and trust Him, not only in blessing but in silence, in struggle, in surrender.**

How does this scene reveal the growing intensity of this woman's faith?
- She begins at a distance, crying out her request to this God-man she had surely heard could heal with a word. She could have become discouraged as her cries were met with silence, as she overheard the disciples imploring Jesus to send her away. Was she less worthy than many who had received healing at His hand? She could have turned back. Instead . . .

- She remains. Her daughter is bound by darkness, and she believes Christ can set her free. At last, Jesus speaks. His words offer no encouragement—only a reminder that she is outside the bounds of His mission. She could have felt dismissed. Instead . . .
- She drew closer. She falls before Him in worship, still pleading for help. Even then, His reply could have wounded—a statement that seemed offensive and unkind. She might have walked away in pain or pride. Instead . . .
- She remains low, her faith unwavering. She lives the cry of Job, "Though He slay me, I will hope in Him" (Job 13:15). With humble heart, she receives His words as true. Yes, Lord. Truly, Lord. Even so, Lord. She claims no entitlement, but delights in the crumbs of mercy, knowing even the smallest gift from His hand is more than she deserves.

There was much Christ could have complimented this woman for—her wisdom in dialogue, her humility in receiving His words, her patience in waiting. But He singled out one thing: her faith. The Lord never rejects weak faith, but He does delight to honor great faith.

What About You?
How do you respond when it feels like your prayers hit the ceiling, when answers are delayed, or when God tells you no? If you have grown weary, disheartened, or angry at God, remember this story and others like it. Let the lives of those with unshakable faith teach you how to stand. Are you in a season of testing? Praise God for the opportunity to exercise Your faith. Is the Enemy whispering lies? God doesn't care . . . You're forgotten . . . If He loved you, He wouldn't be so cruel. Silence him with truth. Draw near to God. Worship Him, especially when it is hard.

Pray
Lord, make me more like this Canaanite woman. When answers are delayed and silence lingers, help me to trust that You are still good. Give me wisdom to discern when to yield to Your "no" and when to keep seeking You for the desires You've placed in my heart. I know I deserve nothing from Your hand, yet You are kind and merciful and have gone to great lengths that I might approach Your throne with confidence. When Your answer tarries, let me not grow discouraged, but wait with hope and perseverance, believing You are at work. Give me courage to keep my eyes on You and a heart that worships You no matter what. Truly, You are the strength of my heart

and my portion forever. **Make me unceasing in prayer and mature my faith through the hardships that are bound to come.**

"Sing praises to God, sing praises; Sing praises to our King, sing praises" (Psalm 47:6).

- "Somewhere in Your Silent Night" by Casting Crowns (2017)
- "Though You Slay Me" by Shane & Shane (2013)
- "Have Thine Own Way, Lord" by Adelaide A. Pollard (1907)

Notes

_____

_____

_____

_____

_____

_____

_____

_____

_____

_____

_____

_____

_____

53

Day 14
The Woman Caught in Adultery: Defined by Mercy

Read John 8:1–11.

Imagine this spectacle: A sacred space pierced by shame. A woman caught in the very act. Disheveled hair. Partially clothed. Tear-stained face drenched in fear. Prideful men spewing venomous judgment. Curious crowds pressing in. And there, the Savior—the One sent to redeem—stooped over, tracing lines in the sand. What was He writing? What answer would He give?

The Pharisees cared nothing for her; she was a pawn in their trap. If Jesus spared her, He would defy the law of Moses. If He condemned her, how could He claim to be the friend of sinners, beloved by the people? Christ would soon carry the weight of her sin. Her life was held in His grace. **She was brought before the just Judge, the only One who perfectly embodied justice and mercy.**

How does Christ illuminate the scene with love, wisdom, and mercy without forsaking justice?
- How heavy must her shame have weighed beneath the glare of accusing eyes. Stooping down in the midst of this heated moment seemed an intentional act to shift attention away from her trembling shoulders onto Himself.
- Oh, the wisdom in His response to the Pharisees! Such a gentle statement that brought conviction to even the hardest of hearts. We are called to gently restore, not humiliate, sinners (Galatians 6:1).
- God's sovereign hand worked through the evil intent of these Pharisees. Sin, long hidden in the shadows, sears the conscience and hardens the

heart. As her sin was brought into the Light, grace unfolds, and she is given an opportunity to repent and be made new.

- How deep was His mercy to her, His words not of condemnation but salvation. Jesus did not come into the world to judge and condemn but to save (John 3:17).

Jesus does not excuse her sin, nor does He affirm her in it. Notice this: Scripture never names her "the adulterous woman." That title, often stamped upon her by commentators, is absent from the heart of God. He does not define her by her failure. Her sin is not her name. Her shame is not her identity.

What About You?

Is there secret sin hidden in the corners of your life longing to be brought into the light? How much gentler the way of humble confession—bringing it before a trusted brother or sister—than being exposed in shame, dragged unwillingly before the throne. Who might walk beside you, pray with you, as you seek to forsake a particular sin? Don't delay. Or perhaps you know one who is caught in sin's grip. Do you view them with condemnation, eyes clouded with judgment, because you don't struggle with that same sin? If so, lay that attitude down. Confess it. Ask God to show you how you might carry their burden and help guide them home with gentleness. Where do you find your identity? In your sin? In "your" righteousness? Let it be anchored to Christ alone. Let Scripture shape your understanding of yourself. Begin a list of the names and truths Christ's Word speaks over you. Add to it as truth is revealed and return to it often to be reminded.

Pray

Lord, thank You that, like this woman caught in adultery, I am defined not by my sin but by Your mercy. You came to fulfill the law, and You did so perfectly. You are indeed a friend of sinners. I don't know if the woman embraced the gift You offered that day and chose to follow You, but I have. Thank You for the times You have made my heart sorrowful over my sin and granted me repentance. Let my heart never grow hard that I lose sight of my need for You. Thank You that my sin no longer names me, that You have made me new. Teach me who I am in You, and help me walk by Your Spirit and in the beauty of new of life. As I celebrate the miracle of Your coming, let me never forget why You came: to rescue, to redeem, and to restore. The cradle pointed to the cross. **Thank You, Jesus, for bearing the**

punishment I deserved and showering me with mercy.

"Sing praises to God, sing praises; Sing praises to our King, sing praises" (Psalm 47:6).

- "I Heard the Bells on Christmas Day" by Casting Crowns (2008)
- "Sweetly Broken" by Jeremy Riddle (2007)
- "Stricken, Smitten, and Afflicted" by Thomas Kelly (1804)

Notes

_____

_____

_____

_____

_____

_____

_____

_____

_____

_____

_____

_____

_____

_____

_____

Day 15
A Man Blind from Birth: Glory on Display

Read John 9:1–38.

How fascinating to watch this encounter unfold. At one point this man was speaking with Jesus and had no idea who it was he was talking to. How often the nearness of Jesus escapes our notice. Though his eyes were closed to the world, he was never hidden from the sight of the Savior. This man who had never in his life seen the light of day, when his eyes were opened, had the pleasure of gazing upon the Light of the World.

This man had lived his days a poor, blind beggar—each morning unfolding like the one before, marked by the same dusty road, the same outstretched hand, the same silence from unseen skies. This day began no differently as he sat hoping for scraps of mercy from those passing by. But by sunset, everything had changed, for on this day he came face-to-face with Christ. He who once begged now bore witness. How could he keep silent? **His life became a living echo of Psalm 96:3: "Tell of His glory among the nations, His wonderful deeds among all the peoples."**

What is the progression of glory this man gives to Jesus?
- First, he obeyed Jesus. Matthew Henry noted, "Those that would be healed by Christ must be ruled by Him."[1]
- Then, he testified, telling his neighbors and leaders of the wonders Christ had done.
- He recognized Jesus as prophet, a man filled with the Spirit of God.

---

1 "John 9 Matthew Henry's Commentary," n.d., accessed July 1, 2025, https://biblehub.com/commentaries/mhc/john/9.htm.

- When pressed to deny the truth, he stood firm. The Pharisees tried to smother the light, but he had encountered the Light of the World, and he would not be silent.
- With boldness, he challenged the religious authorities who brazenly opposed the truth.
- He recognized and confessed that Jesus was from God.
- And at last, he believed in his heart and confessed with his mouth that Jesus was Lord and worshipped him.

Because he was resolute in glorifying God, he willingly bore the cost of allegiance to Christ. Though the Pharisees excluded him from fellowship in the temple, they had no power to exclude him from fellowship with Christ.

What About You?

Is God's glory on display in your life? If you are a child of God, His Spirit dwells in you. Christ is near to you. You are seen by the King of the universe. Let these truths shape your steps and season your speech. Do you feel resistance from anyone in your life because of your faith? Don't let that silence you. Speak boldly of the wonderful things He has worked in your life. Rejoice if you are counted worthy to suffer for His name. Once, you were blind and poor. Now you see. Now you are rich with a heavenly inheritance—imperishable, undefiled, unfading, kept in glory for you. So whom can you tell today? Draw near to Christ. Delight in His presence. Lift your voice in worship.

Pray

Lord, make me more like the man who was blind from birth. I want to be willing to suffer for Your name, that Your glory might be displayed in and through my life. I rejoice that I am seen and known by You; I rejoice that You have opened my eyes to behold You as the Way, the Truth, and the Life. Empower me to walk in obedience, no matter what You would ask. As I celebrate You as the Light who came into the world, let Your light shine through me so clearly that others might be moved to glorify You. Give me courage to speak boldly, even when I face opposition and persecution. **Open my mouth to declare Your praise and tell of all the wonderful things You have done in my life!**

"Sing praises to God, sing praises; Sing praises to our King, sing praises" (Psalm 47:6).

- "In the First Light" by Travis Cottrell (2008)
- "Heart Full of Praise" by Phil Wickham (2021)
- "To God be the Glory" by Fanny Crosby (1875)

Notes

_____

_____

_____

_____

_____

_____

_____

_____

_____

_____

_____

_____

_____

_____

_____

_____

Day 16
Mary of Bethany: At the Feet of Jesus

Read Luke 10:38–42 and John 11:28–35; 12:1–8.

We encounter Mary three times in the Gospels, and each time we find her at the feet of Jesus. Mary shared a profound intimacy with Christ and had trust that was deeply rooted in Him. Jesus often visited Mary and her siblings at their home in Bethany, enjoying refreshment through their hospitality and friendship.

Mary knew Jesus as her defender. When rebuked by her sister and later condemned by Judas, she remained quiet, trusting Him to speak on her behalf—and He did. Mary knew Jesus as her teacher, her comforter, her Messiah. **Knowing Him intimately brought her to His feet in devotion, time and time again.**

What is the significance of Mary's position at the feet of Jesus?
- It was the posture of a disciple. In a world that rarely made space for women to learn, Mary took her place with quiet boldness. She sat with her heart and mind fully fixed on Jesus. Unmoved by the flurry of daily demands, she chose the better portion—to listen, to learn, to linger—and Jesus would not take that away from her. Wisely hungering for heavenly rather than earthly things, she received commendation from her Lord. He honored her decision to seek His kingdom first.
- It was the posture of brokenness. When sorrow struck, her brother lying in the grave, Mary rose at the sound of Jesus's summons. Leaving behind the comforters, she ran to the Comforter. Falling at His feet once again, she poured out her grief, even her confusion. "If You had been here," she said through tears (John 11:32). Jesus did not rebuke her disappointment. Instead, He received it, wept with her, and stood in tender solidarity with her sorrow. He met brokenness with tender

compassion.

- It is the posture of sacrificial service. In one final act of love, Mary came bearing costly perfume—perhaps the most precious thing she owned. She broke the jar and poured it out in offering and adoration. Letting down her hair in public, violating social and religious norms, she anointed her Lord for burial. Though some scoffed and scolded, Jesus called it a beautiful thing, a good work prepared by God Himself. While others counted coins, Mary counted Him worthy of everything.

At the feet of Jesus, Mary both gave and received. She gave her attention, devotion, all that she was, all that she had; in return, she received wisdom, comfort, assurance, protection, and favor from the lover of her soul. As she humbled herself to honor Christ, He exalted her.

What About You?

Do you often find yourself at the feet of Jesus? Have you experienced the deep intimacy with Him that comes from fixing your eyes, ears, and heart on Him? Open the Word of God today expectantly, asking Him to reveal Himself more fully. Choose the better portion—seek His kingdom first. Are you suffering? Is your heart aching over something God could have changed but didn't? Bring those wounds to Him in honest prayer. He will meet you with comfort and work all things for good in His time. What work has Christ ordained for you today? You may not have His physical presence as Mary did, but He tells us, "Truly I say to you, to the extent that you did it to one of these brothers of Mine, even the least of them, you did it to Me" (Matthew 25:40). Serve Christ by serving others. Give and receive at His feet today.

Pray

Lord, make me more like Mary of Bethany. May I often be found at Your feet, abiding in the tender nearness of Your presence. As I sit with You, let my knowledge of You grow and my love for You deepen. Mold my heart so that it is a place You are delighted to dwell. Reorder my desires until nothing rivals You; You are my portion now and forever. Your ways are higher than mine and so hard for me to understand at times. Help me to trust that You are working all things together for my good and Your glory. What meaningful work do you have in store for me today? Keep me in tune with Your Spirit and open my eyes to those You would have me serve. Thank

You, Jesus, for tearing the veil and inviting me to Your throne of grace. **Draw me there to Your feet day after day, moment by moment.**

"Sing praises to God, sing praises; Sing praises to our King, sing praises" (Psalm 47:6).

- "How Many Kings" by Downhere (2008)
- "Captivate Us" by Watermark (2006)
- "Fairest Lord Jesus" by Friedrich von Spee (1677)

Notes

_____

_____

_____

_____

_____

_____

_____

_____

_____

_____

_____

_____

Day 17
Martha: A Servant's Heart

Read Luke 10:38–42 and John 11:18–28; 12:1–2.

Poor Martha—nearly always overshadowed by her sister, remembered more for her worry than her welcome. We exalt Mary's stillness and sigh at Martha's striving, hearing again the Lord's gentle rebuke. Yet if we look more closely, we find something precious: Jesus loved Martha—not in spite of her busyness but perhaps even because of it.

The sisters of Bethany appear to be women of means, able to offer hospitality with grace and abundance. Their home became a haven, a place where Jesus often found rest. Martha, though mistress of the house, did not cling to comfort or status. There, in the melody of kitchen toil, her devotion pulsed just as surely as Mary's did in stillness. **With sleeves rolled and hands busy, she labored in love, humbly serving those she welcomed in—Jesus among them.**

What strengths shine through Martha's seeming weakness?
- Hospitality. With open doors and generous hands, Martha welcomed many with little notice. Her table was set with kindness, her home a refuge. Jesus never reproved her for serving—only for letting the weight of her service pull her heart away from Him. She strove for extravagance when simplicity would have sufficed.
- Faith. When death cast its shadow, Martha didn't hide in sorrow—she rose to meet Jesus. Her grief did not turn her from Him but drew her closer. Though her heart was aching, her words spilled out with strength and confidence, "Yes, Lord; I have believed that You are the Christ" (John 11:27). Her confession echoed Peter's (Matthew 16:16), a revelation Jesus declared to be born not of flesh but of heaven.
- Kindness. Yes, once, Martha had tried to pull her sister away from

Christ, but in their time of greatest pain, she leads her to Him. Once, she had questioned Jesus's care; now she reflects it. In her healing, she gently calls Mary to the Healer. What deeper kindness is there than bringing a broken, wounded soul to the feet of Jesus?

Martha continued to serve, but with a quieter heart. She didn't abandon her calling after Jesus's gentle reproof; she refined it. No longer burdened by distraction or worry, she learned to serve not merely for Him but with Him—in step with His will, less burdened by the weight of the world.

What About You?

Do you feel the tension between serving Jesus and simply sitting with Him? If you find yourself more like Martha, don't be discouraged! Remember: Jesus loved Martha dearly and delighted in her hospitality. He never asked her to stop serving, only to remain near as she did. How might you serve with both attentiveness to your guests and presence with Christ? Perhaps it means offering a simpler table, adorned with peace instead of perfection. Does your soul resonate with Martha's bold confession, "Yes, Lord; I have believed that You are the Christ, the Son of God, even He who comes into the world"? That same Christ now lives in you. Let that anointing flow through you as you serve, and may every act of kindness gently point others to Him. How can you keep your focus on Jesus as you serve today?

Pray

Lord, make me more like Martha. Teach me to be faithful in service yet ever aware of Your presence. Let me not be pulled away by the trivial or the urgent but anchored in what is eternal. Quiet the noise within me so I may hear Your voice, even amid the clatter of tasks and the rhythm of daily life. Align my heart with Your will, that my priorities would reflect Yours. When others gather in my home during this season and always, may I continually seek You and follow Your leading, so my guests feel not only welcomed by me but embraced by You. As I serve, may my heart remain peaceful and fully present. Let Holy Spirit fruit flow through me and the fragrance of Christ linger in every room. **Show me how I might usher those around me into Your presence as I serve them.**

"Sing praises to God, sing praises; Sing praises to our King, sing praises" (Psalm 47:6).

- "Give This Christmas Away" by Matthew West (2011)
- "Lifesong" by Casting Crowns (2005)
- "O Master, Let Me Walk With Thee" by Washington Gladden (1879)

Notes

_____

_____

_____

_____

_____

_____

_____

_____

_____

_____

_____

_____

_____

_____

_____

_____

69

Day 18
Woman Healed on the Sabbath: Unbound to Give Glory

Read Luke 13:10–17.

Though burdened by eighteen agonizing years of suffering, the woman still came to the temple on the Sabbath—drawn by a quiet hope to encounter God there. Though the synagogue official dismissed her as insignificant, Jesus spoke otherwise, insinuating she was more valuable than an ox or a donkey, animals that were held in high esteem in biblical times. The ox, steady and strong, was the backbone of the fields—plowing earth, sustaining life, and central to the sacred offerings of the temple. The donkey, humble yet tireless, bore heavy loads, carried traders and farmers alike, and marked the wealth of its owner. Both animals were guarded by God's own laws, to be cherished and protected.

Jesus noticed this woman and declared her worth. He called to her. She could have turned away, ignored His invitation, hardened her heart against hope. Instead, she responded by drawing near to Him. He lifted her body and her spirit up with one touch of His merciful hands. In that moment, the weight of years fell away—pain surrendered to healing, bondage gave way to freedom. **In her newfound freedom her heart poured forth praise, unable to contain the glory of God who had touched her and made her whole.**

What contrasts dance in this woman's story before and after the touch of the Savior?
- Bent over to erect. Her body bowed low, eyes fixed upon the dust, weighed down by years of helplessness. But Jesus lifted her, straightening spine and spirit alike. In that instant, her gaze soared heavenward, and praise burst from her lips.

- Bound to released. Chained by a cruel infirmity, she had been held captive by a power not her own. Satan's grip was tight, but not tighter than the hand of Jesus. With one word, He broke her bonds and set her free.
- Sick to well. For eighteen long years, healing eluded her. She was powerless to escape her affliction. With unrivaled power and authority, He restored this daughter of Abraham.

The Enemy comes to steal, kill, and destroy. Lifting up, freeing, healing—these are the sacred works of God, life poured out in abundance.

What About You?

Have you carried a burden so heavy it feels endless, an ache that stretches beyond all hope? Does the enemy of your soul hold you fast in unseen chains? Have you grown weary, believing the cruel lie that God neither sees nor cares? Dear child of Abraham, hear this truth: He sees you. You are precious, deeply loved, held close to His heart. Take courage. Turn your face toward Him. Draw near and rest beneath the gentle touch of His hand. Watch and wait—see how He will move in your midst. Even if you have pleaded a thousand times before, will you persist and once again ask for the freedom and healing only He can offer? Watch for His answer, your spirit eager to burst forth in praise when it comes.

Pray

Lord, make me more like this woman who was healed on the Sabbath. Though, and even because, I endure much suffering in this life, may I continually seek Your holy presence. May I always remain faithful in suffering and steady in hope. Thank You that You consider me valuable, that You notice me, that You see my suffering, that You bottle my tears. I come to You now, trembling yet expectant. Touch me with Your mercy; lift my chin so I may look into Your face. I turn to You now ready to respond, to receive, to be made whole. Release Your power into my life and free me from the chains of the Enemy. Restore what has been lost; rebuild what has been broken. **Help me to walk in newness of life, to move with freedom and purpose, and let every breath and every step bring glory to Your name.**

"Sing praises to God, sing praises; Sing praises to our King, sing praises" (Psalm 47:6).

- "Hark the Herald Angels Sing" by Amy Grant (1983)
- "When I Think About the Lord" by Rita Springer (2007)
- "And Can It Be That I Should Gain?" by Charles Wesley (1738)

Notes

_____

_____

_____

_____

_____

_____

_____

_____

_____

_____

_____

_____

_____

_____

Day 19
The Cleansed Leper: Heart of Gratitude

Read Luke 17:11–19.

Leprosy—an incurable, disfiguring affliction—slowly devoured the body and marked the soul as cursed. It was seen as a sign of divine disfavor, a sentence to isolation and an agonizingly slow death. Lepers were cast out, cut off from the life they once knew, forced to dwell on the fringes of both society and hope. In all the pages of the Old Testament, only two are recorded as healed: Miriam, who bore the disease briefly as a rebuke, and Naaman, a foreign general whose healing came through humble obedience. For most, healing was a dream too distant to chase.

These ten lepers, when they saw Jesus, called Him Master, a word of surrender, of trust. They stood at a distance, as the law demanded, yet their hearts leaned in. Jesus told them simply, "Go and show yourselves to the priests" (v. 14)—the only ones at the time who could declare them clean and restore them to community. He asked for no proof, gave no instant cure, yet in His command was a promise. Though their skin still bore the marks of decay, they obeyed. Step by step, as they moved in faith, healing met them along the way. Nine went on, eager for restoration. But one—the outsider, the Samaritan—turned back. Before he claimed the fullness of his healing, he returned to the Source. He fell at Jesus's feet, giving thanks, offering glory, before he went on to receive the full benefit of his healing.

How did this one leper differ from the other nine?
- All ten cried out in desperation, their voices raised in pleading prayer, "Master, have mercy!" Only one returned with a voice lifted in praise, glorifying God with the same passion that once fueled his plea.
- All ten kept their distance, unclean and unworthy, petitioning Jesus from afar, the unclean not coming too close to the Pure One. Only one

closed that gap in humility, offering humble praise at Christ's feet.

- This one Samaritan, an outsider, overflowed with gratitude, while the other nine, presumably sons of Abraham, vanished into restored lives without returning to the Giver.

Through this moment, Jesus revealed the width of His mercy—the gospel reaching beyond borders and bloodlines, drawing near to the lowly, the outcast, the grateful heart. Many cry out in distress and receive God's mercy; few acknowledge the Giver of the gift.

What About You?

Have you found yourself in a predicament you couldn't solve on your own, faced with a challenge impossible to conquer? Have you known the sting of isolation—whether by your own choices or wounds you did not choose? Perhaps even now some corner of your life aches with that loneliness. Cry out to God, the Healer, the One who restores bodies and minds, hearts and homes. Listen for His voice, and be ready to follow, even when the path forward seems impossible. Trust His wisdom and move in faith. When He answers—when grace meets you on the way—don't rush on. Return. Lift your voice in grateful praise. Let your thanksgiving be joyful and loud. Be among the rare few who remember not just the gift but the Giver, who offer Him the honor He so richly deserves.

Pray

Lord, make me more like the cleansed leper. May I always overflow with gratitude, be quick to return, eager to fall at Your feet. I have so much to thank You for! I was wandering a road that led to ruin when You reached down from heaven and breathed life into my soul. Now I long to walk in step with Your will, to respond to Your voice with faith and obedience. Though I feel like an outcast in this world at times, You, the King of the universe, have welcomed me as Your own and called me beloved. Thank You!!! May Your praise always be upon my lips. Jesus, I am so weary and frail at times; revive and strengthen me according to Your Word. Renew all that is broken in my body, mind, and spirit. Make me ever watchful for Your hand at work, ever quick to give You glory. You have answered more cries than I can count and given more gifts than I can name. **May my life be a living thank-you, an offering of worship to You.**

"Sing praises to God, sing praises; Sing praises to our King, sing praises" (Psalm 47:6).

- "Noel" by Lauren Daigle (2016)
- "Jesus, Thank You" by Sovereign Grace Music (2005)
- "O Worship the King All Glorious Above" by Sir Robert Grant (1833)

Notes

_____

_____

_____

_____

_____

_____

_____

_____

_____

_____

_____

_____

_____

_____

_____

Day 20
Bartimaeus: Persistent Faith

Read Luke 18:35–43.

Amid the opulence and bustle of Jericho sat a blind beggar. Jesus was "passing by" (v. 37). His time there would be short. This moment held the promise of salvation. The crowd surged forward, blind in their own way—blind to compassion, blind to the heart of the One they followed. They imagined the Messiah would be too grand to stoop to the cries of a beggar. How often the multitude misconstrues the Messiah! The throng urged Bartimaeus to silence, but with a spirit as fierce as a tempest, he raised his voice all the louder. He cried out, his plea a beacon of unyielding faith, defying the world's clamor.

As he called out, his unseeing eyes turned toward the Light of the world, hoping for a miracle, believing the One who could heal. "Son of David," he cried, a title rich with meaning, acknowledging Jesus as the Anointed One. Amid the noise, Jesus paused. The cry of true faith never goes unheard; it will always turn the head of the Savior. Though on His way, though the multitude pressed in, though this man was overlooked by the world, Jesus stopped for this solitary voice of faith. **As the beggar's plea for mercy pierced the air, it spoke of his understanding not just of Christ's power to restore his sight but of His ability to renew his very soul.**

How do we see Bartimaeus's faith unfold?
- Upon learning that Jesus was near, he lifted his voice in a bold appeal for mercy, confident the One passing by had the power to help.
- As the crowd sought to stifle him, his plea only rose louder and more resolute.
- When summoned by the Healer, he obediently drew near without hesitation.

- When standing face-to-face with the Savior and invited to share his desire, he poured out the deepest longing of his heart.

We encounter Bartimaeus as a blind and destitute beggar seated on a dusty road. Through his encounter with Jesus and his unwavering faith, we witness a remarkable transformation. No longer just a beggar in rags, Bartimaeus is revealed for who he truly is: a beloved child of the King, known by name, lifted by grace, and called to follow the Light.

What About You?
Has the crowd around Jesus, those who should lead you toward Him, ever pushed you away? The sting of rejection can weigh heavy, wounds inflicted by those bearing His name but missing His heart. Perhaps you bear the scars of church hurt. Will you respond like Bartimaeus, steadfast in your gaze upon the Savior, seeking His mercy even when others attempt to silence you? To Christ you are precious—seen, known, and deeply loved. What is it you seek from Him today? He beckons you to come as you are, not polished or perfect, to bare your heart. Be specific. Let your faith arise, believe in His boundless power, and dare to utter a bold prayer today, trusting in the One whose power knows no limits and whose mercy never fails.

Pray
Lord, make me more like Bartimaeus. Give me a persistent faith that rises above impossible circumstances and the cold dismissal of the crowd. Let my gaze remain fixed on You; let my hope sink deep roots in Your goodness and compassion. I believe You are the Almighty God. Nothing is too difficult for You. These mountains in front of me can crumble in an instant by one word from Your mouth or one touch of Your mighty hand. You are my help, my strength. My soul clings to You, and Your right hand upholds me. Heal the wounds caused by Your people. Help me always to walk in grace and forgiveness, focusing on Your goodness rather than the hurt I have endured because of their failings. **When I call out to You, I trust You to respond with perfect love, to shape me into Your image, and to adorn my life with the beauty of Your mercy.**

"Sing praises to God, sing praises; Sing praises to our King, sing praises" (Psalm 47:6).

- "He Has Come for Us (God Rest Ye Merry Gentlemen)" by Meredith Andrews (2017)
- "Open the Eyes of My Heart Lord" by Michael W. Smith (2001)
- "Be Thou My Vision" by Eleanor Hull (1912)

Notes

_____

_____

_____

_____

_____

_____

_____

_____

_____

_____

_____

_____

_____

_____

_____

Day 21
Zaccheus: Overcoming Obstacles

Read Luke 19:1–10.

Here we continue in the bustling city of Jericho, where traders and travelers converged, streets busy with commerce and commotion. A man named Zaccheus, small in stature but rich in influence, stood amid the crowds. His name, meaning "pure" or "innocent" in Hebrew, seemed a paradox against the backdrop of his profession as a chief tax collector. In this position, Zaccheus wielded considerable power and amassed great wealth, much of it certainly stained with exploitation. Beneath his polished exterior and the coins he counted, a deeper hunger stirred that all the silver in the world could not satisfy.

His soul's longing found its answer that day as Jesus glanced toward him. Jesus, always the Alpha, always the initiator. Their eyes locked on one another, the Savior's gaze piercing through layers of guilt and pretense. This moment of divine connection sparked a profound transformation within Zaccheus, who responded with promises of repentance and restitution. Jesus had called forth the new man—a death sentence for the one stained with ambition and sin. The encounter not only altered his path but also promised a ripple of grace that held the power to touch his entire household, his city, and perhaps beyond. **With unwavering determination, Zaccheus had surmounted every barrier to catch a glimpse of the Savior.**

What obstacles did Zaccheus overcome to fix his eyes on Jesus?
- External factors. Casting aside his dignity, he ran ahead of the crowd that blocked his view, undaunted by the jeers such a spectacle might draw.
- Personal limitations. In another undignified act, he ascended a tree to see above the crowd despite his height.

- Cultural norms. Zaccheus, undeterred by the murmurs of a judgmental crowd enshrouded in legalism, cast aside their scorn to embrace the grace of Jesus.

Zaccheus's spirit, once tethered by greed and self-interest, soared free in the light of Jesus, holy and perfect. Despite his unworthiness, he eagerly swung wide the doors of his heart and home to welcome the sacred fellowship Jesus requested.

What About You?

Do you long to catch a glimpse of Your Savior, to see Him more clearly, to know Him more deeply? What shadows obscure your view of His glory? Perhaps the murmurs and judgments of others form unseen walls that block your view. Maybe feelings of inadequacy cloud your vision. Is the world around you drawing a veil over your eyes? Ask the Lord to lift these burdens, to guide you past every hindrance, until Your heart beats in rhythm with His. What binds you and prevents you from tasting the sweetness of divine communion? Is there a sin weighing you down, from which you can turn in repentance? Take a moment now to invite the Lord to search the depths of your heart, to uncover any hurtful habit that lingers in the shadows. Let His light shine there. The Lord is calling you to fellowship. Determine to overcome every obstacle to fix your eyes on Him.

Pray

Lord, make me more like Zaccheus. Kindle within me a holy fire, a burning desire to see You, to behold Your face above all else. May the opinions of others fade into insignificance as I earnestly seek Your presence. Through intimate fellowship with You, transform me. Clear the path before me; remove obstacles that cloud my vision of You. Clearly show me what hinders my pursuit and grant me the courage to lay it down. Illuminate the hidden shadows in my heart, guiding me toward repentance and the joyous freedom of Your forgiveness. As I remember how You left the glory of heaven to step into homes and hearts here on Earth, I am moved with gratitude that you have chosen to dwell in me despite my failings. Lead me in mending the wrongs I have committed, that I may walk in the light of Your truth. My soul yearns for unbroken communion with You. Thank you for welcoming me into Your presence despite my imperfections. **I am determined, no matter the cost, to cast aside every barrier and focus my gaze on You.**

"Sing praises to God, sing praises; Sing praises to our King, sing praises" (Psalm 47:6).

- "Here Comes Heaven" by Elevation Worship (2018)
- "Jireh" by Maverick City Music (2021)
- "Jesus Paid It All" by Elvina M. Hall (1865)

Notes

_____

_____

_____

_____

_____

_____

_____

_____

_____

_____

_____

_____

_____

_____

_____

Day 22
The Poor Widow: Simple Faith

Read Mark 12:41–44.

Just before this quiet moment in the temple, Jesus issued a sobering warning about the scribes—those who exploited the very ones the law was meant to protect. Among the most vulnerable in ancient Israel were widows, left without husbands to shield and support them in a patriarchal world. Yet Scripture tells us that God Himself is a defender of the widow (Psalm 68:5).

When the God of the universe begins a statement with "Truly I say to you," we would do well to lean in and listen. A teachable moment for the disciples is a teachable moment for us. Picture the widow's offering—two tiny coins—resting beside the lavish gifts of the wealthy. Her miniscule contribution bore the weight of true sacrifice, unlike their abundance given without hardship. Jesus did not condemn the rich for what they gave, but He did highlight the greater value of this widow's contribution in comparison. He noticed. He always notices. **Beyond the coins, He saw to the heart of simple faith that surrendered them.**

How do we see this poor widow quietly living out her faith?
- What could two small coins possibly achieve, offered in support of the grandest structure in Israel? And yet she entrusted them to God, believing even the smallest gift was not too small in His hands.
- She sought first His kingdom with this act of sacrifice and devotion, casting aside the worries of this world, entrusting herself to God's faithful provision.
- She wasn't intimidated by the spectacle around her: the wealthy, the noise of their offerings, the grandiosity. She gave anyway, what she could, in simple devotion.

Her modest gift, unnoticed at the time by all but Jesus and his disciples, is remembered today by believers across the ages.

What About You?

As you offer your time, talent, or treasure, do you imagine Jesus seated nearby, watching not with scrutiny but with love? He weighs not the size of the gift but the heart that offers it. He doesn't ask for grand displays, or compel you to give from guilt, but invites you to give with joy. He honors what is offered in quiet faith, when no one else is watching. Do you feel your sacrifice is too small to make a difference? Our God brings abundance from scarcity. Do you cling to worldly possessions, fearing insufficiency if you let go? Remember: You are infinitely valuable to your heavenly Father who will provide for your every need. Do you compare your offering to that of others? Lift your eyes to Jesus. He is your focus, your audience, your reward. Ask Him what offering—be it small or grand—would bring delight to His heart and yours today. Place it in His hands. Let it rise like incense, a beautiful act of worship, pleasing to the One who sees beyond the tangible to the depths of your heart.

Pray

Lord, make me more like the poor widow. Help me to trust You completely, freeing me to hold nothing back from You and the work of Your kingdom. When I feel my offering is too small, remind me of Your power to do magnificent things with my humble gifts. After all, You are the One who formed the world with a word, the One who filled vessel after vessel with oil from the widow's single jar, the One who fed thousands with five loaves and two fish. May my gaze remain fixed on You, untainted by comparisons. Help me to live with open hands, that I might freely receive and give as You desire. May my giving be devoid of pomp and infused with joy; knowing You see is enough for me. What can I bring to You today that would delight Your heart? **As Your workmanship, my desire is to walk the path of simple faith embracing the good works You have prepared for me.**

"Sing praises to God, sing praises; Sing praises to our King, sing praises" (Psalm 47:6).

- "What Child is This" by Third Day (2006)
- "Abide" by Aaron Williams (2021)
- "I Surrender All" by Judson W. Van DeVenter (1896)

Notes

_____

_____

_____

_____

_____

_____

_____

_____

_____

_____

_____

_____

_____

_____

_____

89

Day 23
The Penitent Criminal: Repentance Without Regret

Read Luke 23:32–43.

There is a worldly sorrow that leads to death, that crushes hope beneath its weight. We see this in Judas. Stricken with remorse when he saw Jesus condemned, he cast away the silver and then his life (Matthew 27:3–5). Regret without redemption leads to a bitter end.

But there is another sorrow—a sorrow shaped by the hand of God. This is the story of the penitent thief. All around, the Son of God is scorned: Religious leaders sneer with smug delight; soldiers mock like children playing with power; and two criminals, guilty and condemned, join in the jeering. Matthew tells us that even the penitent one once hurled insults with the rest (Matthew 27:44). But something changed. Perhaps it was the divine moment he heard Jesus pray for His executioners: "Father, forgive them" (Luke 23:34). **Grace shone into a darkened heart, leading not to despair but to repentance without regret—a sorrow that saves.**

Awakened to grace, how do we see the blossoming of repentance in this man's soul?
- He feared God, recognizing true holiness beside him.
- He confessed guilt, owning his sin and its just reward.
- He proclaimed Jesus's innocence, a Lamb unblemished in the midst of wolves.
- And finally, he turned—not away in shame but toward the Savior—and simply asked, "Jesus, remember me" (Luke 23:42).

His work, like ours, was this: to believe. God's grace immediately followed.

His deathbed became a doorway securing his eternal place in the presence of Jesus.

What About You?

Did you, once upon a time, catch a glimpse of Jesus that softened your heart of stone? Like the penitent thief beside Him, have you seen the radiant holiness of God and, in that light, recognized your own need and turned to Him for rescue? The fact you have read this far suggests you have. But know this: That turning isn't meant to be a single moment in time. Repentance—a sincere, attentive turning from sin toward God—is meant to be the rhythm of a believer's life. Ask God to search your heart and mind, to reveal any lingering regrets you cling to. Turn to Him again and lay them down in honest surrender. Allow Him to fill your open hands with forgiveness, healing, redemption. Now, in this moment, what promise is He inviting you to trust, to hold close, to believe anew today?

Pray

Lord, make me more like the penitent criminal, ever aware of Your holiness and my deep, desperate need for Your mercy. Let me never forget that the baby in the manger was also the King on the cross. Forgive me for the times I have fallen in with the crowd and failed to honor You with the reverence You deserve. Thank You for the countless ways You have softened, shaped, and molded this wandering heart. Even in my stumbling You have been so patient, faithful to chisel away all that does not belong. Lead me to the promises, the transformational truths, tucked within Your Word, and by them, conform me ever more into Your likeness. When I stray from Your will and Your ways, may guilt never drive me to despair but stir within my heart a godly sorrow that draws me back to You. **Jesus, Light of the World, shine into the depths of my heart and reveal any darkness hidden there so that I might turn to You in true repentance.**

"Sing praises to God, sing praises; Sing praises to our King, sing praises" (Psalm 47:6).

- "King Of Kings / Angels We Have Heard On High" by Maverick City Music (2021)
- "Beautiful Scandalous Night" by Robbie Seay Band (2007)
- "There is a Fountain Filled With Blood" by William Cowper (1772)

Notes

_____

_____

_____

_____

_____

_____

_____

_____

_____

_____

_____

_____

_____

_____

_____

_____

Day 24
Joseph of Arimathea: Faith Unveiled

Read John 19:38–42.

Matthew tells us Joseph was a wealthy man, that it was in his own rock-hewn tomb that he would eventually lay the bruised and broken body of the Savior (Matthew 27:57–60). Mark reveals him as a respected member of the Council, a man who, though surrounded by opposition, found the strength to rise above fear. With quiet resolve, he "gathered up courage" and went to Pilate and asked for the body of Jesus (Mark 15:43). Luke describes him as good and righteous, a man of integrity whose conscience would not allow him to concur to the unjust verdict (Luke 23:50–51).

Finally, John reveals another detail: Joseph was a secret disciple of Jesus because he feared the Jews who had promised to put anyone out of the synagogue who acknowledged Jesus as Messiah (John 9:22). Collectively, these descriptions paint a picture of a man of wealth, influence, virtue, and quiet devotion. His simple expression of loyalty played an eternally significant part in the unfolding of the kingdom he awaited as he fulfilled the prophecy spoken hundreds of years earlier in Isaiah 53:9: "He was with a rich man in His death." **As the apostles cowered in the shadows, this once-hidden follower cast off his secrecy and displayed his faith for the world to behold.**

What barriers had to be overcome to bring this disciple into the light?
- His wealth. It is hard for a rich man to enter the kingdom of heaven (Mark 10:25). The temptation to place one's hope in riches rather than in God is strong (1 Timothy 6:17).
- His prestige. The wise, powerful, and well-regarded are not often the ones who heed the call of the gospel (1 Corinthians 1:26).
- His fear. Scripture is silent on how he "gathered up courage," but fear

rarely falls without a fight.

Love triumphed over fear as Joseph stepped out of the shadows bearing the weight of grief and grace, carrying the broken, lifeless body of his soon-to-be-risen Savior. Though Jesus was crucified as a criminal, He was, thanks to Joseph, buried like a King.

What About You?
Have you found yourself a secret disciple—silent in certain circles, cautious with your convictions, careful not to disrupt the comfort of the crowd? Is it time to gather up courage and let the light of Christ shine through you regardless of how people might respond? Will you ask God to breathe fresh boldness into your faith today? Ask Him to make you unashamed of the gospel that saved you. Ask Him to help you rise above any fear of man. Are there other barriers holding you back—riches that glimmer with false promises, a hunger for reputation that eclipses your true calling, or comforts that lull you into quiet compromise? Nothing is too difficult for God. Not your fear. Not your past. Not even the tangled loyalties you have come to depend on. Today, ask God for boldness. Seek to honor Christ even if it means your devotion will be on public display. Let your light shine before men!

Pray
Lord, make me more like Joseph of Arimathea. Teach me to lay down all things that hold me back from complete devotion to you. Forgive me for the times I have been ashamed to acknowledge You, that I have succumbed to silence and let fear keep me from speaking Your name. Let the overflow of my heart become a mouth that can't stop proclaiming Your goodness and truth. Thank You for Your endless mercy and patient love, the way you gently lead me as You grow my faith. Make me unashamed of the gospel, for I know it holds the power of God. Reveal to me anything that quietly wars against my complete trust in You. Dig up roots of resistance and prune away that which does not bear fruit. **Give me the courage to stand firm, speak truth, love boldly, and reflect Your light in a world that is desperate for hope.**

"Sing praises to God, sing praises; Sing praises to our King, sing praises" (Psalm 47:6).

- "Wonderful" by CAIN (2021)
- "Reason I Sing" by Phil Wickham (2021)
- "Jesus, I My Cross Have Taken" by Henry Francis Lyte (1825)

Notes

_____

_____

_____

_____

_____

_____

_____

_____

_____

_____

_____

_____

_____

_____

_____

_____

Day 25
Two on the Road to Emmaus: Hospitality to a Stranger

Read Luke 24:13–36.

In the simple gesture of extending hospitality, we may, as the Word of God declares, welcome angels into our midst unaware. But these two? They welcomed the risen Son of God Himself. Though their hearts were heavy with sadness, they still found room for kindness. Their conversation was rich with the story of Jesus—of the One crucified, now mysteriously near. To the man they believed a stranger, they spoke with reverence: He was "mighty in deed and word before God and all the people" (v. 19). Even in grief, they offered fellowship. And what a blessing it became.

Because of their invitation, a fog of doubt gave way to the fullness of faith. Christ walked with them, not only on the road but through the corridors of their hearts—searching, stirring, leading. As they accepted their daily bread from the hand of Christ, their eyes were opened, their hearts set ablaze with His light. Disappointment gave way to glory. Where once they hoped for a nation's redemption, they now beheld the Redeemer of all. Jesus promises to come in when we open the door to Him (Revelation 3:20). **With gentle grace Jesus drew near, and these men eagerly extended warm hospitality.**

How do these two men welcome this "Stranger"?
- They offered Him fellowship on the dusty road, sharing the road and their thoughts.
- In humility, they received His words as He unfolded and illuminated the Scriptures before them.
- As Jesus pretended He would walk on, they urged Him to stay. They

had experienced the pleasure of communion with Christ and longed for more.

Christ had made Himself known to these men through His Word and at His table. Joy ignited their steps as they rushed back to Jerusalem to share the good news.

What About You?

Do you welcome friends and strangers into fellowship? When you open your door to a stranger, the Lord says you invite Him in. As the glow of the Christmas season fades into ordinary days, continue to make room for the Bread of Life. Ask Him to reveal Himself to you in His Word—to teach you, to stir you, to help you understand. Allow Him to kindle a flame in your heart that moves you deeply as you behold the vastness of God's love. Speak of his death and resurrection as these two did. Let your conversations be lit with the gospel—when you sit at your table, when you walk along the path, when you lie down to rest, and when the sun rises again. Share His good news wherever your feet carry you and with whomever God places in Your path. Do you recognize Jesus in the breaking of the bread at the Lord's table, in this sacred meal that makes the gospel visible? Leave all distractions behind as you come to His table. Ponder its meaning. Experience His nearness. Invite Him in.

Pray

Lord, make me more like the men on the road to Emmaus. May my heart remain tender and my door always open to friends and strangers alike. Let me never miss the quiet knock of someone in need. More than anything, I pray that You would always feel welcome here—in my home and even more so in my heart. Let nothing in me resist Your nearness. Thank You for the gift of Your fellowship; there is no joy more profound than communion with You. Thank you also for the gift of fellowship with others whom You have woven into my walk with You. As I open Your Word, illuminate my mind to understanding. Grant me a spirit of wisdom and revelation in the knowledge of You. Wherever my hope is too small or has wandered off course, redirect me in truth. Cause my heart to be aglow and overflow with Your love. May every word I speak carry echoes of Your goodness. As I sit at Your table, shoulder to shoulder with Your people, may I not take this sacred privilege lightly. **May I always eagerly extend hospitality to You and to every soul You love.**

"Sing praises to God, sing praises; Sing praises to our King, sing praises" (Psalm 47:6).

- "O Come, All Ye Unfaithful" by Bob Kauflin (2020)
- "Psalm 34" by Brooklyn Tabernacle Choir (2018)
- "Break Thou the Bread of Life" by Mary A. Lathbury (1877)

Notes

_____

_____

_____

_____

_____

_____

_____

_____

_____

_____

_____

_____

_____

_____

Appendix
Manger to Mercy Display

This display can be created simply and inexpensively or as elaborately as you like. Because one of my goals in all of this was to simplify, I chose to keep things simple and affordable. I hired a young man from our community to build the cradle and cross. He crafted them from old pallets to keep the cost low, and the result was beautiful in its humble, rustic charm.

Throughout the year, I collect and create small gifts to fill the manger—treasures found at yard sales, thrift stores, dollar bins, or gathered from my garden. I also love using resources from Mountain Rose Herbs (https://mountainroseherbs.com/) to make simple DIY gifts with herbs and essential oils.

I use three different styles of wrapping paper—one for adults, one for kids, and one for all ages—along with two ribbon colors to distinguish between male and female gifts. A simple key helps guests easily identify which gifts are best suited for them. I attach gift tags with the appropriate Bible verse to each of the gifts as a hint as to what might be inside. I tuck wrapped gifts into the manger, and as friends and family visit throughout the season, I invite each one to choose a gift.

Each day beginning December 1, I read a devotion and hang that day's ornament on small nails I have placed along both bars of the cross. By the end of the season, it's adorned with beauty—each ornament a quiet testimony, a reminder of those who were saved and transformed by the grace and mercy that was purchased for them there.

Materials needed for Manger to Mercy display:
- Manger
- Cross with 25 small nails or hooks
- An ornament to represent each devotion
- Wrapped gifts with Bible verse attached

Gifts ideas for manger (italics added for emphasis):

- Activity books: "A man of understanding will acquire wise counsel, to understand a proverb and a figure, the words of the wise and *their riddles*" (Proverbs 1:5–6).
- Candy: "O *taste and see* that the LORD is good; How blessed is the man who takes refuge in Him!" (Psalm 34:8).
- Cards or board games: "Everyone who competes in *the games* exercises self-control in all things. They then do it to receive a perishable wreath, but we an imperishable" (1 Corinthians 9:25).
- Chapstick: "Because Your lovingkindness is better than life, *my lips* will praise You" (Psalm 63:3).
- Christian devotionals: "This is eternal life, *that they may know You*, the only true God, and Jesus Christ whom You have sent" (John 17:3).
- Coffee mug or teacup: "*My cup* overflows" (Psalm 23:5).
- Herbal tinctures: "By the river on its bank . . . will grow all kinds of trees for food . . . their fruit will be for food and their *leaves for healing*" (Ezekiel 47:12).
- Flashlights or candles: "I am the *Light of the world*; he who follows Me will not walk in the darkness, but will have the Light of life" (John 8:12).
- Gloves: "So I will bless You as long as I live; I will lift up *my hands* in Your name" (Psalm 63:4).
- Gratitude journal: "In everything *give thanks*; for this is God's will for you in Christ Jesus" (1 Thessalonians 5:18).
- Honey sticks: "How sweet are Your words to my taste! Yes, *sweeter than honey* to my mouth!" (Psalm 119:103).
- Mini perfume oils: "For we are a *fragrance of Christ* to God among those who are being saved and among those who are perishing" (2 Corinthians 2:15).
- Mini raisin boxes: "Sustain me with *raisin cakes*, refresh me with apples" (Song of Solomon 2:5).
- Pillow spray: "In peace I will both *lie down and sleep*, for You alone, O LORD, make me to dwell in safety" (Psalm 4:8).
- Prayer journal: "*Pray* without ceasing" (1 Thessalonians 5:17).
- Salt scrub: "You are the *salt of the earth*" (Matthew 5:13).
- Socks: "How beautiful are *the feet* of those who bring good news of good things!" (Romans 10:15).

Acknowledgments

As always, my deepest and most heartfelt thanks belong to God. He is the One who sovereignly allowed the circumstances that stirred my heart to resist the status quo. He is the One who whispered the invitation to something new. It was on my early morning prayer walks and at His feet in His Word that the words for this book came to be. Thank You, Father—this is Yours.

This was a stealthy project. Until the very end, even those in my own household didn't realize I was working on another book. To them it looked no different than my regular time in Scripture. And yet, James, Ian, and Adrianna, thank you for living unconstrained by cultural expectations. I love that our home is a place where people are free to be who God created them to be and to walk in the calling He's placed on their lives.

Mom, thank you for always being my greatest cheerleader. Long before my first book was published, you were already proclaiming to the world how eager you were to read the next. Your belief in and support of me has meant more than words can say.

Deb Hall, my editor—what a gift you are. You do far more than correct grammar. You help untangle my scattered thoughts, gently root out repetition, and give shape and clarity to what my heart longs to say. Thank you for helping my words sing.

Lili, thank you for giving me a crash course in Adobe In Design! Tackling the formatting on my own was a bit maddening at times, but so satisfying.

To all of you I thanked in *Off with the Old, On with the New*—those words still ring true. They always will.

"I will sing to the Lord, because He has dealt bountifully with me"
(Psalm 13:6).
God has blessed me greatly through all of *you*. Thank you!

Thank You for Reading
Manger to Mercy: Portraits of Grace!

I'm truly grateful for your feedback—your insights help shape not only future editions of this book but also any books yet to come.

If this book encouraged or inspired you in any way, would you take two minutes to leave a review on Amazon? I'd love to hear your thoughts. Your words matter more than you know!

Visit my website at www.stephanieripple.com to join my newsletter and download free resources designed to enrich your journey through *Manger to Mercy: Portraits of Grace.*

Thanks so much!
—Stephanie Ripple

www.ingramcontent.com/pod-product-compliance
Lightning Source LLC
Chambersburg PA
CBHW060644130626
46555CB00002B/952